Endorsements from those who have experienced public persecution:

We encourage you to read *Like a Flood* if you are serious about being ready to stand firm for Jesus when the pressure to compromise hits your life! This is a dynamic tool to help you, your family, and your church withstand the dark flood with confidence by being a part of the courageous flood of hope and spiritual light.

—The Benham Brothers, David and Jason
Business Entrepreneurs and Best-selling Authors
of *Whatever the Cost* and *Living Among Lions*

I found out the hard way that persecution for your faith in America is very real. *Like a Flood* is a powerful tool to prepare your family to stand firm for Jesus in the midst of increased pressure. I highly recommend you read it and then give a copy to your friends and family.

—Lana Rusev
Wedding planner and owner of Simply
Elegant Event, Jacksonville, FL

Endorsements from Pastors and Christian leaders:

This book, *Like a Flood*, is a must read for everyone. I wish every American everywhere had it in their hand right now. America is in deep trouble spiritually, financially, socially and globally. Lisa does such a great job at addressing some of the most crucial issues with not only clear explanation but with solutions that are tangible and can be executed immediately. This book will equip you and encourage you to once again be found in the spirit of America and the beautiful Christian roots of our dear country. Many people are confused and even more are fearful. The pages of this book will bring you strength and courage. It will inspire you and reconnect you to the great truths of the King of Kings. Our future can be bright. Lisa will ~~help you see this and prepare for it.~~

— D

Bishop, ?K

President, Livin ?H

D1111543

Great reading! Lisa speaks from a background of once being liberal. Knowing Lisa's personal story, she has an urgency to awaken people to see that the liberal agenda seeks to unravel the fabric of strength that holds our nation together and makes us a great nation. Lisa's book is an "on time" word and "wake up call" to Christians as she gives the former hidden agenda into how our nation became what it is today. A nation whose government was originally established with purpose using principles from the Bible and today has purposefully thrown away those principles. Lisa doesn't stop there just describing the problem, she gives us answers how to rise up and take back ground that was stolen from us. She challenges us, as the majority in our nation, to rise up and take action together instead of letting a small group continue to try to intimidate us. I believe, as Lisa does, that God isn't finished with our country. This book will motivate you to get up and do something, to become engaged with others in turning our nation back to God.

—Pastor Sharon Daugherty
Victory Christian Center
Tulsa, Oklahoma

Lisa Cherry does it again! *Like a Flood* is a clarion call to the body of Christ to take it's rightful place, to live boldly, to love without restraint and to raise up a standard of Godliness. I pray that as you devour this book you are inspired to be apart of a tidal-wave of goodness that leads lost and hurting people back to Him. This book is a necessary reminder that the Church is without a doubt truly the hope of the world!

—Kemtal Glasgow
Pastor | Family Life Ministries
Gateway Church, Southlake, Texas

Like a Flood offers prophetic insight into today's cultural challenges coupled with practical application to equip believers how to stand in a culture that vilifies them. Cherry's message is exactly what the body of Christ needs right now to be informed, emboldened, and prepared to rise up like a flood against the enemy!

—Linda Seiler
Director, Chi Alpha Christian Fellowship
Purdue University

Lisa is a wealth of knowledge and continues to amaze me with her wisdom and knowledge from a Christian perspective. *Like a Flood* contains a message that each living breathing individual needs to read. These pages contain a profound reminder of whose we are and what we are called to live out on this earth here, now, today. This is a must read that raises a much needed awareness for the body of Christ. It is a call to stand on the front lines with fervency, conviction, and passion and to reclaim America with boldness and strength. *Like a Flood* imparts key information that is life changing and ushers in a keen awareness of what needs to happen in order to turn this sinking ship around.

—Lauren Kitchens-Steward
American Family Radio Host,
College Professor, and Inspirational Speaker

This is a passionate, inspiring challenge, combined with practical application, to help us impact individuals and a nation to return to spiritual sanity and godliness. It is a well-documented assessment of our current condition, yet contains a hope-filled strategy for believers to rise up and shine into darkness! Our church greatly benefitted from the *Like a Flood* event. I highly recommend it to other pastors and leaders.

—Ronnie Holmes
Pastor, Church of the Open Door
Waco, Texas

As a local pastor my heart is to prepare my congregation and my family to stand firm in the middle of great cultural turmoil and darkness. *Like a Flood* is a now word for us. It is a practical tools inspire as well as challenge believers to live joy-filled and fruitful lives. Please make this book a priority read for you, your family, and your church.

—Pastor Victor Torres
New Wine Fellowship
Waterford, MI

Lisa writes with clarity and focus, addressing issues in our day that many are tempted to ignore. She is gifted at articulating what we need to hear to help us shine as lights for Christ in these challenging times!

—Pastor Bruce Payne
Calvary Campus Church
Carbondale, IL

Lisa Cherry's book is a clarion call to open our spiritual eyes and take action in view of the changing reality in our culture. We are in the midst of a life and death struggle for this generation and how we respond will define what we become. I pray as your read *Like a Flood*, you will be challenged, as I was, to ride the wave of God's flood of hope and revival.

—Pastor Ephraim Garcia
House of Restoration Ministries
Staten Island, NY

We have been part of a group of parents meeting at our church for over three years. Frontline Family Ministries has been tremendous for all of us in strengthening the focus on Christ in our homes. At a time when our culture continues to become more nonsensical, *Like a Flood* is an outstanding resource for us as we stand strong for Jesus.

—Darin and Rebekah Zehr
Parents & Church Leaders
Lowville, NY

LISA CHERRY

LIKE A FLOOD

LIVE **BOLDLY.**
LOVE TRUTHFULLY.
STAND **FEARLESSLY.**
IN A POST-CHRISTIAN
AMERICA

HONOR✠NET
PUBLISHERS
Sapulpa, OK

ISBN: 978-1-938021-38-1

Published by HonorNet
P. O. Box 910
Sapulpa, OK 74067

To my family
Lucas, Rebekah, Hannah, Micah, Matthew,
Ethan, Lydia, and Josiah
Nathan, Tara, Lilibeth, Ryan, Ben, and Andrew
Adam, Kalyn, Kyla, and Elijah
Earl, Sandra, Beth, and Jeff
John, Aveniel, Diane, and Bob.

And most especially to my husband, Doug.

Thanks for being a part of my ark-building team!

I love you all very much.

FOREWORD

As Christians we are called to reach out with compassion to all people with the love of Christ while resisting with courage the agenda set against our freedoms and faith. In the book *Like a Flood*, Lisa Cherry refers to this agenda as a flood. A flood that is sweeping away the Christian foundation of America and seeking to redefine what it means to be followers of Christ. She encourages us to stand firm in our faith against the flood and undertow of secular sin, confusion, and spiritual darkness that is coming like a tidal wave against everything it means to be Christian.

While we enjoy the tremendous blessings of being grafted in to the Vine, there are times when Christians are called to fight for the faith—moments when God tells us to stand up and step into the battle between good/evil, truth/lies, and light/darkness.

As brothers, professional athletes, entrepreneurs, and most of all, Christians, we know firsthand how intimidating the flood of culture can be. We had our national TV show cancelled due to us choosing our faith over our TV fortune (laugh). Like Lisa, we felt supernatural courage to run *to* the battle and not *from* it.

Life isn't easy—it's a fight. As Jude says in the Bible, I felt the necessity to write to you appealing that you contend earnestly for the faith which was once for all handed down to the saints (see Jude 1:3). If you're a contender, that means you're a fighter. Unfortunately, when it comes to the faith, many Christians don't know they're contenders and aren't ready to fight. They have bought in to the lie that good Christians "get along" and accept whatever the world hands them, including defining what it means to be a good Christian. Lisa, in this book, exposes the secular agenda and provides us a clarion call to stand up as followers of Jesus and not be conformed to this world as Paul writes about in Romans.

If we are contenders of the faith, we cannot be conformers of this world. *Like a Flood* shows us that we are the standard that God is raising up in this time.

We are the holy flood that will stand up for what is right, true, and virtuous for the purpose of His Glory in all the earth. God always has a plan, and that plan is us. What an awesome privilege and incredible responsibility!

We encourage you to read *Like a Flood* if you are serious about being ready to stand firm for Jesus when the pressure to compromise hits your life! This is a dynamic tool to help you, your family, and your church withstand the dark flood with confidence by being a part of the courageous flood of hope and spiritual light.

—THE BENHAM BROTHERS, DAVID AND JASON
BUSINESS ENTREPRENEURS AND BEST-SELLING AUTHORS
OF *WHATEVER THE COST* AND *LIVING AMONG LIONS*

TABLE OF CONTENTS

PART ONE
FLOOD #1: THE DARK MESS

PART TWO
FLOOD #2: THE BEAUTIFUL FLOOD OF HOPE

PART THREE
THE PREPARATION PLAN

INTRODUCTION

God is looking for the courageous in this hour: leaders in homes and churches, marketplaces and schools; ordinary people who are eager to stand for righteousness when others are running or hiding from truth. Perhaps that is why this book fell into your hands today.

Today there are two floods sweeping over America: The first is a dark wave sweeping the land and rewriting the landscape of our collective lives. It is loud and persuasive as it peddles lawlessness and uncleanness that mocks at our God as it uproots long held boundaries and rewrites standards of norms. But it is also a whole lot more.

The second flood is of a totally different nature. Born of the Spirit, its holy hope-infused power is not as well recognized or talked about yet. It is what Isaiah 58 calls the standard. And where it rolls, the first flood is interrupted and made to bow. Its supremely powerful force is so unbelievably beautiful that those who get swept away by its power will not be paralyzed by the dark flood that tries to discourage and distract! Let's be real. We are living in unbelievably crazy times. So crazy we need a scorecard to keep up with the outlandish changes. And I, for one, am alarmed. Are we, His children, really ready for this assignment to live in a post-Christian America?

That is why I decided to write this book. My family and I needed some clear, down-to-earth help, and I figured you and your family and friends did too. Surely you know what I am talking about.

Daily the dark flood overwhelms our senses, mocking us as if it cannot be stopped. Our internet feed screams odd incongruences:

> Do not check that box male or female on Facebook just yet. There are now fifty-eight gender options listed for you to choose.[1]

> I am all for women's rights. I am also for the free practice of Islamic law too.[2]

> Selling baby body parts that have been dismembered in an abortion is not barbaric. It is actually humane, you know?[3]

> No problem. Whichever gender you feel you are today, let us know, and you can go to that assigned gender's bathroom.[4]

> It's just natural. I am a Christian, and I am gay. The Bible doesn't ever say that is a problem.[5]

> People who oppose homosexuality are bigoted haters! Throw them into jail for discrimination…or better yet, just bomb their houses.[6]

> Capitalism is enslaving the world. We need to get those big businesses to pay more taxes.[7]

And we wonder to ourselves: Am I somehow in the middle of a new sci-fi movie where the whole world has taken a crazy pill? Does anyone else notice those ideas mentioned above are conflicting and make no sense? But then we look around, and we whisper, what is God's plan in the middle of this dark flood mess?

And He answers by pouring out His own flood.

Some would propose that all hope for America is gone. We are post-Christian with only judgment ahead. While still others would say talking about America misses the whole point anyway. The real issue they say is the end of the age with the second coming of Jesus imminently at hand.

So which view is correct?

Well, I, like most of you, have spent quite some effort trying to figure it all out! And my conclusion is…I do not know for sure. And I am not sure if anyone else really knows for sure either.

So I figure we can all become paralyzed analyzing that question. Or we can rephrase the question to one that seems more fruitful to the issues at hand:

> Lord, the dark flood is obvious.
> But we need Your wisdom in this hour…
> What should Your children do now?
> Isn't that the bottom line question in our hearts?

I am grateful for all the highly trained apologists and theologians who can wax eloquent, explaining all of the complex problems of our day. We need them like never before. But, quite frankly, many of us have not prepared ourselves as we know we should. In this book we will explore simple yet profound principles of truth that will equip us, our family, our friends, our small groups, and our churches in this critical hour.

Like a Flood is divided into three strategic parts. In Part One, "The Dark Mess," we will explore the terrible flood that has forced us to recalibrate life in a post-Christian America. As we peel back the curtain of lies, we will expose the deceptions that are pulling us down.

Part Two is titled "The Beautiful Flood of Hope." You are going to love this section. It is here we discover the unbelievably awesome power flowing from God's throne to those who are ready to honestly face the dark flood in Part One. Please do not read one part without the other unless you want to miss the fullness of the message!

Part Three is where the message of *Like a Flood* gets very practical. It is titled "The Preparation Plan." In this section I have identified twenty-four answers to our question: What should we do now? This list of preparations, when applied diligently, will mature us and cause us to discover the joy that our Father yearns for us to have even now in the midst of the flood.

I believe He has something special in store for us as we share time together in these pages. This is the hour of His mercy toward all who have hearts to receive. So while we still have time, while there is still light enough to see, let's listen together to what He is saying to His children in *Like a Flood*.

PART ONE

FLOOD #1:
THE DARK MESS

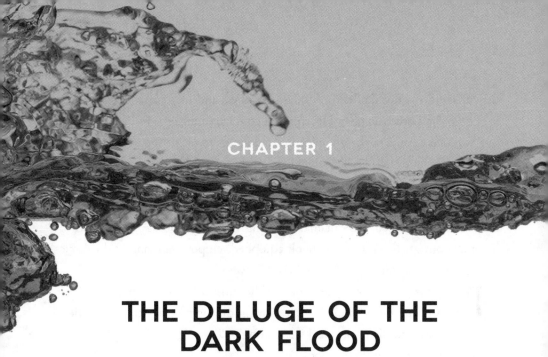

CHAPTER 1

THE DELUGE OF THE DARK FLOOD

Silence in the face of evil is itself evil: God will not hold us guiltless. Not to speak is to speak. Not to act is to act.[1]

—Dietrich Bonhoeffer
Pastor and speaker of truth in Nazi Germany

I worried about starting this book with talk about the dark flood. Who wants to read another doom and gloom book when we already feel discouraged? I thought about inverting the order of the book and giving you the awesomely great news about the second flood first and then backdooring you into the deluge of the dark flood.

But just as the cross came before the resurrection and law came before grace, the second flood will only make sense after we wrestle with the reality of the first dark flood.

We are living at a Dietrich Bonhoeffer moment of decision. The American church is poised to respond to the greatest challenge she has ever faced. Just like our German brothers during Hitler's reign, we need leaders who will help us withstand the hostile flood of today's darkness and help us rediscover fierce loyalty to the Lord who gives His children courage to make right decisions.

I will make you a deal. You give me six chapters to tackle the tough issues of the darkness, and then I will share with you some of the most exciting news of your life. That is a fair trade, don't you think?

You can probably already tell I am a straight shooter. I will give you vital information you need without manipulating your emotions. And I intend to leave us both at the end of this book equipped, empowered, and enthusiastic about our next season together as Christ followers.

Writing this book proved to be one of the most difficult and most glorious experiences of my life. I found myself moving through a crazy transformation of attitudes toward the project as I went along.

First, I needed to write this book.

Then, I felt called to write this book.

Then later, I was burdened to write this book.

But finally I was desperate to write this book.

Why? Because in these pages are revelations that I believe can transform all of our lives.

So as we open this first chapter, get ready to meet the dark flood.

June 23, 2015

Obergefell v. Hodges.[2] I suppose that phrase will eventually roll off my tongue as easily as *Roe v. Wade.* But on that day the words seemed foreign, awkward, and strange. In fact, those odd names seemed so clinically removed from my own personal life that I would just try to forget them if I could.

But I couldn't.

Obergefell v. Hodges

The final pronouncement from the highest court of our land.

The end of a string of legal judgments that would make all other announcements obsolete.

It was official. Marriage had been legally "re-defined." Five judges had done what most had thought could never really happen.

And it was if in the middle of my living room I could hear the rain pick up force.

I took to my news feed to sort out the stories.

The scene on the steps of the Supreme Court Building was clear. Celebration. Flags. Colors and banners touting the newly coined phrase *Love Wins*. I knew it was an image I would remember the rest of my life.

But my heart skipped a beat. As I watched the drama unfold, questions arose in my heart. Did love really win that day? Was this really the dawn of a new era of freedom, or was this the beginning of something unchartered and ominously dark?

Were we to be celebrating that day or mourning?

Anticipating or dreading?

Lifting up praise to our heavenly Father as some were publicly doing, or falling to our knees as others in humble intercession?

The words of three of the dissenting Supreme Court justices rang in my heart.

> If you are among the many Americans—of whatever sexual orientation—who favor expanding same-sex marriage, by all means celebrate today's decision. Celebrate the achievement of a desired goal. Celebrate the opportunity for a new expression of commitment to a partner. Celebrate the availability of new benefits. But do not celebrate the Constitution. It had nothing to do with it.
>
> —Justice John Roberts[3]

> Inversion of the original meaning of liberty will likely cause collateral damage to other aspects of our constitutional order that protect liberty.
>
> —Justice Clarence Thomas[4]

> At present no one, including social scientists, philosophers, and historians, can predict with any certainty what the long-term ramifications of widespread acceptance of same-sex marriage will be. And judges are certainly not equipped to make such an assessment.
>
> —Justice Samuel Alito[5]

The strange euphoria in the streets stood in obvious contrast to the other side of the opinion box. I took to social media to see what others would say.

There was Susie and John. Two Facebook "friends" who were among the first to light up their faces in the rainbow flag. Oh, that did not surprise me. They had flown their colors in many heated arguments on that page before. But then there was Angie. And Philip. And Marie. And then Anna Claire and her brother too.

The flag over their faces made no sense as I struggled to decode what they were trying to say. Oh yes. Anna Claire has a cousin who came out of the closet as a homosexual last year. So I guess that is why her family was celebrating the new view.

But what about Philip and Marie and Angie? What had changed with them from when we were hanging together at church? Why were they making a declaration that I would have never thought they would say?

And then over my shoulder I was sure I heard the sound of the rain growing stronger, hitting on the windows above me in the den where I sat.

As evening fell on my musings, my teenagers rolled into the house waving their phones in front of my face, "Mom, have you seen the White House? It is lit up like a rainbow! How can the President do that, Mom? Do you think it is a Photoshop job like some people claim…or is it possible it is really true?"

Any other day I would have laughed them off as pranksters. But this was no joke. No laugh. And no cute festive trick. We (my government and I) were making a statement for the world to see. But I, for one, was looking at the rainbow colors…but also hearing another voice speaking impressions in that secret place of my inner heart.

Lisa, you are right. The rain is now pouring. It is not just tapping on your window in a steady pitter-patter that beckons your attention if you feel like attending to its sound. This is different. The very atmospheric condition has shifted. It is storming. It is pouring. It is flooding across your land.

Make no mistake about it. The deluge is here.

It is real. It is strong. Much stronger than you have ever known. Get ready for its engulfing force. It will wipe out anything not anchored in its path. Get ready to shift into the new season of life here on earth. Oh, many may scoff at these words. Many will think you crazy. Outdated. Alarmist. An unloving, judgmental fool. But don't be confused. That is their choice. You must get ready to be misunderstood and get ready to see Me respond.

Like a flood.

The Flood Defined

My own personal experience with flood waters is limited to a brief surge of water that backed up in the basement of my childhood home and a flash flood that blocked a few streets in my hometown. Nothing too remarkable.

I have only observed floods at a distance on The Weather Channel. Uprooted trees. Moved landscaping, shifted roadways, and a wall of water that takes everyone by surprise. These are the images of a flood of significant proportions.

The flood in America started as a steady trickle. But now the trickle has given way to the powerful water wall. I have heard these words for years from people in churches all over the United States. . . .

I just can't believe how quickly the world has changed.

I don't even want to watch the news and see what is happening.

I am so sad. This is not the America I want my kids to know.

I just do not know where to start protecting my home.

I don't know what to do when my teachers and professors are pressing me to think their way.

But now, we are at Weather Channel drama level. Let me illustrate with just a few of the recent headlines in case you need a reminder.

Ashley Madison: Possibly Millions More Christians Have Committed Adultery Than Previously Thought

My pastor Is On the Ashley Madison List

ISIS Kidnaps Dozens of Christians From Churches

Report: Obama Posts Pro-Abortion Nun, Transgender and Gay On Pope's Welcoming Committees

Porn Warps Young Minds, Leads to Violence, Study Finds

California Votes to Make Assisted Suicide Law of Land

Children's Publishing Giant Scholastic Pushes Pro-Transgendered Kids Book

"Call Me 'Ze,' Not 'He'": University Wants Everyone to Use "Gender Inclusive" Pronouns

Despite Barbaric Videos, Most Americans OK Planned Parenthood Funding

This Pro-Abortion Lawyer Told Congress That Dismembering Babies Is "Humane"

"Burn Kim Davis Alive"

New ISIS Video Vows a Repeat of 9/11 Terror to America

School Now Pushing Soft Porn for Tweens, Islam for All Kids

Miley Cyrus: Belief in Noah's Ark Is "Insane"[6]

It is all so overwhelming…like a flood. And those were just the headlines from one news site for a period of a few weeks. This flood is coming so quickly and strongly now, it feels as if I could fill this book with new material every day and still my list will look dated to you whenever you read it because so many big things will have happened in between!

The Source of the Flood

John S. Dickerson wrote about this dark flood in his 2013 book *The Great Evangelical Recession*.

In the coming decades United States evangelicals will be tested as never before, by the ripping and tearing of external cultural change—a force more violent than many of us expect. Evangelicalism in the United States has stood strong through centuries of difficulties and setbacks. She has not seen anything quite like what she will see in the next fifty years.[7]

Now wait a minute. Fifty years of pressure? That is quite a long season of storm surge flood! Dickerson goes on to make four crucial observations about these flooding conditions:

1. The broader "host" culture of the United States is changing faster than most of us realize.

2. The direction of that change includes pro-homosexuality and anti-Christian reactionism.

3. The rate of the cultural change in this direction will further accelerate as the oldest two generations die, taking their traditional "American values" and votes with them.

4. These changes will reach a point at which they directly affect the church as we know it and our lives as individual evangelicals.[8]

Lest we think that Dickerson's prediction is an isolated report, please note how his sentiments are echoed by other leaders in the body of Christ.

> We have crossed an invisible line and there are no signs that we are capable of turning back. Like a boat being caught in the mighty torrent of the Niagara River, we are being swept along with powerful cultural currents that just might put us over the brink. Seemingly irrevocable trends put in motion forty years ago continue to gather momentum and speed. Our Judeo-Christian heritage that gave us freedoms we have enjoyed is for the most part gone, and in its place is an intolerant form of humanism that can boast of one victory after another. The "culture war" we used to speak about appears to be over and we lost.[9]
>
> —Dr. Edwin Lutzer,
> Longtime Pastor, Moody Church

> The ramifications of this decision [*Obergefell v. Hodges*] are seismic. Proponents will seek to drive Christians and Christian institutions out of education at all levels; they will press laws to force faithful Christian institutions and individuals to violate consciences in work practices and myriad other ways.[10]
>
> —Matthew C. Harrison
> Missouri Synod Lutheran President

While we affirm our love for all people, including those struggling with same-sex attraction, we cannot and will not affirm the moral accept-ability of homosexual behavior or any behavior that deviates from God's design for marriage. We also believe religious freedom is at stake within this critical issue—that our first duty is to love and obey God, not man.[11]

— Ronnie Floyd
President, Southern Baptist Convention

Although it should not be, religious freedom itself is "going to be an issue." In this way, the Supreme Court's ruling regarding so-called "marriage equality" will be used as a wedge to narrow the scope and weaken the protections afforded by the free exercise of religion guaran-teed to Americans by the First Amendment.[12]

—George O. Wood
General Superintendent, Assemblies of God (USA)

America's walls of biblical morality are crumbling. Almost everyone I speak with is distraught over the direction our nation is taking. Christianity and our religious freedoms are under siege. Progressives and secularists want to see God removed from everything and to burn every gate of protection.[13]

—Franklin Graham,
President, Billy Graham Evangelistic Association

Our nation has clearly made a wrong turn. If America's greatness has in any way been tied to our worship of Almighty God and our promotion of godly morality and character, we, by very definition, are in trouble.

But the condition of our nation is only a part of the dark flood story. Over the course of human history, nations come and go. So America's sowing toward wickedness will inevitably create a harvest of wickedness. How horrible! None of us want this to happen.

At the same time, the dark flood upon us may have little to do with America's future per se. The darkness may be the expected result of the prophetic calendar as we move closer to Jesus's appearing. Matthew 24:9–13 describes the condi-tions at the end of the age:

Then you will be handed over to be persecuted and put to death, and you will be hated by all nations because of me. At that time many will turn away from the faith and will betray and hate each other, and many false prophets will appear and deceive many people. Because of the increase of wickedness, the love of most will grow cold, but the one who stands firm to the end will be saved.

So the dark flood may very well be the wickedness Matthew and other scriptures described. If so, we are not promised the conditions we are experiencing now will get any easier! That is why we are exhorted to "stand firm."

The dark flood is graphically illustrated in 2 Timothy 3:

But mark this: There will be terrible times in the last days. People will be lovers of themselves, lovers of money, boastful, proud, abusive, disobedient to their parents, ungrateful, unholy, without love, unforgiving, slanderous, without self-control, brutal, not lovers of the good, treacherous, rash, conceited, lovers of pleasure rather than lovers of God—having a form of godliness but denying its power. Have nothing to do with such people.

Take any of those words apart and note what you have. Disobedient. Abusive. Brutal. Unholy. Is that not a picture of our world today? The dark flood is intense. Its wickedness and lawlessness will be shocking and overpowering so that many believers will wax cold in their love for Jesus. The enticement of the world lures them away. And the threat of the suffering scares them away.

So here becomes our question: Are we ready for whatever our future may hold?

A nation in decline under the judgment of God or. . . .

A world in rebellion to her Creator under the judgment of God.

Neither option seems very comfortable. And yet our God is pulling us toward His heart right now, equipping us to stand firm!

CHAPTER 2

WE ARE STILL NOT READY

The preparations of the heart belong to man.

—Proverbs 16:1, NKJV

1969. That was the year the song "I Wish We'd All Been Ready"[1] exploded onto the music scene of the world's first full-blown Christian rock album. Larry Norman's haunting half-folk lyrics became the fuel for late night camp-fires as young believers sang of things they knew very little about. Children dying. A man and wife disappearing from their bed. The Son coming back and people getting left behind. It was an ethereal storyline that peaked our collective imagination.

1969. That was also the year Hal Lindsey wrote his earth-shaking end times book *The Late Great Planet Earth*.[2] All over America, Christians began preparing for the last dark days before Jesus would return and rapture His church. The discussion was, of course, not without context. The miraculous Six-Day War in Israel certainly had our attention as it seemed the pages of Biblical prophecy were unfolding before our eyes at record speed.

But underneath the spiritual fervor and over-eager anticipation was another force at work also: intense fear.

I was just a kid when rumors of the world ending began circulating around my ears. I remember crying to my mother in terror that I would "not be ready" and end up being one of those casualties in the cryptic song. But honestly, that was not my biggest fear. In my youthful naïveté I think I was more concerned that Jesus would come back before I had a chance to fulfill my girlhood dreams of falling in love, getting married, and having my babies!

But…fast forward almost fifty years and you will notice something incredibly obvious. We are all still here. The end of the world as we know it has not yet occurred. At least not at the time of this writing. And yet my children and now my grandchildren are *still* living under the threat of those dire predictions I heard in 1969:

> Surely these are the Last Days.
> Our nation as we know it may soon fall.
> The world is getting darker and darker.
> Jesus is coming back.
> You must prepare and get ready.

My emotions sometimes wish we could just declare a new narrative line. A song of world peace and not disaster. An announcement that cancels all the doom and magically declares to the world, "Good news! The long awaited crisis of darkness we have been worried about has been averted! We dodged the bullet, and you may come off the alert."

The other part of me knows I cannot do that. Scripture does not support that story line, and the facts around me are also undeniably loud. The days are drawing shorter!

The Dream That Shook Me to the Core

It is not unusual for me to have a dream, but it is unusual for me to have a dream I would want to tell you about. On August 5, 2015 I had a dream that became my own daytime wake-up call. I'm going to do my best to share it with you here. To help you understand the significance of the dream's story line, I have inserted my commentary in *italics*.

Lisa's Dream...

In my dream I had been invited to deliver a keynote message at a major meeting of seasoned pastors and church leaders. It was the event of a lifetime for me. Leaders from all over the world would be in attendance, and somehow I knew my message had the potential to bear major fruit in the Kingdom. So I was both excited and nervous. *We are designed to be fruit bearers (John 15:6). So wanting to be there serving Jesus was good.*

Prior to the evening meeting, I was to have dinner with the head of this prestigious Christian organization. It would be in a meeting room of the convention center complex where this event was to be held. When I arrived for the dinner, I was immediately aware that I was way underdressed for this event. I had prepared myself with a stylish (pop style) outfit from a discount department store when this was clearly a tailored suit event. *Please note: I was dressed in the world's pop style. Trendy, I was dressed to fit in and look cool. I was conforming to the world (Rom. 12:2).*

As we sat together politely visiting over the plate of food prepared for us, I was completely distracted. I was self-conscious about my appearance, but I was keenly aware that my appearance was not my biggest problem. Here I was getting ready for the assignment of a lifetime, and I did not have the message prepared for that night. No notes. No vision. Nothing. I was totally unprepared. *The most important moment of my calling, and I was totally unprepared! What was I doing with my time priorities before this event? What could have possibly been more important than being in God's Word and knowing His message for this important assignment (2 Tim. 2:15)?*

As I carried on my pleasant conversation with the leader, I just kept falsely assuring myself, "Lisa, it is going to be fine. You know there will be three main points to the outline. You will have time to write them down when you are done with dinner." *How presumptuous and arrogant! Like I had all the time to correct my own errors. Such pride (Matt. 23:12). Such self-assurance! Yuck!*

But the longer I sat there picking at my dinner another strange thing started to happen. My hair was falling out of position, sinking from its hairsprayed spot. Ladies, you will know what I mean. It was as if I was mysteriously losing my carefully prepared "hairdo." *Getting caught with my hair down was a brash way of saying the Lord exposed my true inner state (Eph. 5:13).*

The leader was a busy man with a busy schedule so he finished his meal quickly and departed for the convention hall. I was so relieved. I would make a quick exit to run over to my hotel room, change clothes, curl my hair, and most importantly, jot down my notes for the evening event. *Great. Now I would fix my own self (Prov. 8:13). No repentance here was evident.*

The hotel was adjacent to that great convention hall. So I half ran toward my suite and put my key in the lock of the door. But as I reached for the door it pushed open with no resistance. There in my room was a lady I did not know. Then it hit me. Lucas, my son who was traveling with me, must have already checked us out of the hotel. This was no longer my hotel room. *Sometimes while we are distracted the seasons change in life and doors are closed behind us.*

I was frantic. Where was I going to make my preparations now? I did not want to go into the main convention center as my appearance was not even appropriate for the backstage crew. I quickly pulled out my cell phone to call Lucas and arrange for my suitcase to be delivered to the ladies lounge in the outer lobby. *I certainly wanted to keep up my outward appearances, didn't I?*

Now in my dream I was sprinting in panic. One look at the ladies lounge, and I knew I was in further trouble. It was crowded and noisy with ladies primping and chatting on their way to the formal event. It was too late. How was I going to prep my message in that kind of high-stress environment, I mused? *Procrastination. It is usually a form of disobedience to God's timing. So now I would be preparing under a level of stress that God never intended.*

As I waited for Lucas to drop off my suitcase, my hair took another step south. When I looked in the massive mirror, I was horrified. My hairdo was somehow back to my disheveled post-showering look! I looked like a total mess! I tried to hide my head without drawing undo attention to myself. I did not want any of the powder room ladies to know I was their guest speaker. *Can we say "exposed"? I know what I look like post-shower! Ultimate embarrassment. Ultimate humbling coming down!*

My hair and clothes would have to wait though as I grabbed my briefcase to jot down some kind of speaking notes.

At least I was beginning to value the serious mission of delivering the Word of God over fixing my clothes! I tried earnestly to focus my mind at the urgent task at hand.

Think, Lisa, think. What are those three main points you are supposed to speak about? But the harder I thought, the more my anxiety rose, and the less I could think. *The word panic comes from the Greek god Pan. When believers give way to anxiety, we are yielding to the spiritual warfare coming against our minds. I could not think because fear was now my false companion.*

I began frantically praying, "God, what do You want me to say?," when suddenly I got a one-word answer: starfish.

OK. Now this is where it is important to remember this is just a dream. Because in dreamland somehow that one-word answer made sense to me! *Isn't God's grace amazing (2 Cor. 12:9)? Even in my foolish, inept, pride-filled state, He still wanted to use me to speak His Word! That is a crazy kind of Daddy love. I quickly picked up my Bible and grabbed my iPad at the same time. I somehow recognized that "starfish" was in a Bible verse so I googled the verse location. Even in my dream I was using my electronics. Is this good or bad?* That is when my first message point jumped right into my mind:

> Behold, I am doing a new thing; now it springs forth, do you not perceive it? I will make a way in the wilderness and rivers in the desert.
>
> —ISAIAH 43:19, ESV

"Ok. I got it!," I thought. It wasn't three points yet, but at least I had a place to start!

That's when Lucas arrived with my bag. Only it wasn't my bag. I still had no new clothes, and my time was running out. *Can we say desperation here? I wonder how much of my problem was being complicated by spiritual forces of darkness hindering my success.* Unbeknownst to me someone else had been listening to my phone calls and watching me in my dysfunctional bathroom preparations. The ladies lounge attendant approached me with a kind offer of help. "Ma'am, would you like me to get word to the directors of this event that you are running a little late but that you will be there soon?" *Was this lady my angel in disguise?*

"Great idea," I responded, as the intro music for the event and the announcements had already been playing for several minutes.

I was out of options, and I was not sure what to do.

I cannot tell you how overwhelming this sensation of panic was. I was totally out of time. There would be no rescuing my situation. Finally, my lack of preparation had caught up to me, and I was heartbroken and horrified. I literally could not stand the pressure anymore.

And that is when I woke up. Or maybe I should say that is when I woke myself up, as subconsciously the dream had become so traumatic for me I must have known I needed to be rescued.

What Happened Next

Just after I woke up that morning my alarm clock also went off. As it rang it was as if I could hear God's explanation of what I had just experienced. I somehow instantly knew the three points to the message. And I could feel myself in my half-slumber state preaching them in my own head as if it were a special message to me and to you from God's perspective:

> **Point 1:** Behold I am doing a new thing. In every generation I can say that statement. Because I am the creator God. I am calling you to work with My plan. But here is My question to you: Will you really be a part of it?

> **Point 2:** You are not ready. The world has already changed in your midst. You can feel it. You know it. The very atmosphere you are living in is different. The flood waters are rising, and the pressure changes of the flood are revealing a serious flaw. You are not ready to lead in this hour. Just like Lisa in the dream you are floundering around with a half-baked message at the finest hour of your most holy calling. You are dressed in worldly clothes, not spiritual. You have been caught with your hair down when you should have been like the ten virgins in Matthew 25 who were dressed, prepped, and ready. You will not make

it unless you awaken to this fact! But take courage. If you will listen now, you still have time to adjust.

Point 3: You must return to your first love. Do not look to others and tell them they must return to their first love. *You* must return. Do not wait on your pastor, your parishioners, your parents, your children, or your friends. *You* must return to your first love.

I want you to remember how it felt when I was new in your life. The days when you first fell in love with Me. When your salvation was exciting. When your calling was fresh and alive. When we would sit together and dream of the future, not because you were so wise and able, but simply because you were Mine. Return to that simple, connected, and uncomplicated place.

Return to Me on your knees. Talk to Me with the simple passion of a hungry soul. Be My child. Pour out your broken heart and your shattered dreams. They were never yours to carry anyway.

Remember, I am your *first love*.

And then I completely woke up and turned off the screeching alarm. I was shaken so strongly I sat up in bed at full attention. My emotions were electrified, and my spirit was both convicted and encouraged. As I composed myself I began sharing my dream with my husband, when he said the most amazing thing: "Lisa, right as the alarm went off this morning I was also having a dream. I wonder if it might be a piece of your message also?"

Wow, that has never happened to us before! We are not the kind of folks who talk very often about our dreams! Here is what he said: "My dream was about a great flood. I was standing in the middle of our hometown watching waters rising in our streets. Somehow I knew our town was equipped with flood walls around it that were supposed to protect us. But the water all around our town was already about two or three feet high, and those flood walls would not solve our imminent problem. Fortunately, I had a pump that I was confident could rescue the town from ruin. The pump was powerful and adequate for the job, much like an industrial-size version of the sump pump we have under our house." (I knew what he meant because we have had some water drainage issues, and he has had to keep that sump pump in good repair. I personally have never seen the pump as I do not under any circumstances crawl under houses.)

"But in my dream I had a big problem. I could not get that sump pump down in the ground deep enough to do an adequate job. The ground was too hard for it to be placed correctly to operate as it was designed to work. Instead of draining off the flood, it was simply skimming off a little water from the top. I knew my town was in trouble. We were all going to be destroyed." And that was as far as the dream went.

Hard ground is impossible to work with (Hos. 10:12). How tragic that the pump could not be employed! Wow. Doug had a second witness to the themes I believe God was revealing. Can you imagine how much that experience effected my passion for this book? Here is my final summary of what I believe these two dreams were about.

The Two Dreams Explained

Fellow Christians, we are not ready for the pressures ahead. In fact, we are sorely unprepared.

Many of us have been called in this hour. He is expecting us to deliver His Word to others. But we are lazy and distracted and resistant. He has called; we have accepted, but then we have not obeyed in the moments of preparation. We have said in our hearts, "I'll do it later. We have lots of time." We are in for a rude awakening. We may not have a "later."

A dangerous flood of sin is rising in our world. It is threatening to knock many of us off our feet and sweep away many of us with its voluminous flow (Matt. 24:12). And here we are in the church holding the power pumps to deflect the force of the waters, but we find ourselves unable to employ what we know we have. Why? Because we have not done the foundation work so the powerful One can do His work on our behalf. God longs to flow through us to a dying world, but we are filled with arrogant self-dependency and pride. Our soil is hard and crusty. We have moved out of position, and now He is urging us back to His side.

Do you hear Him pricking your heart right now with conviction and urgency to fall to your knees and scream, "God, is that me?" That is what hits my heart as I am sitting here penning these words to the page. I do not want to be caught with my hair down, improperly dressed, and without the Word of the Lord on my tongue! I do not want my pride to keep me from tapping in to the pump of His presence. I do not want to lose the passion of my first love!

Is that how you feel right now even though this was not your dream? Or, are you reading this and you are a little worried that you don't feel the passion that I feel?

You know you should feel it.

And that is the problem.

You have grown weary, dry, cynical, and callused. You have figured that someday you would get ready when the world gets a little more intense. But deep inside you are wondering if something is wrong. Whichever response you just had, I invite you to keep reading.

God is drawing our attention toward Him right now for a purpose. He is giving us another bit of time as He is working in our hearts even now. And if we stick with His voice, I believe we will journey together—changed and ready.

CHAPTER 3

THE RULES CHANGED IN POST-CHRISTIAN AMERICA

Remember ever; and always, that your country was founded…by the stern old Puritans who made the deck of the Mayflower an altar of the living God, and whose first act on touching the soil of the new world was to offer on bended knees thanksgiving to Almighty God.[1]

—Henry Wilson
18th Vice President Under Ulysses S. Grant

It was Easter week in Great Britain, April, 2015. Prime Minister David Cameron, dressed in a professional suit, appeared in a video addressing his fellow British citizens and the rest of the world. Looking pleasantly at the camera, he declared:

Across Britain, we should feel proud to say, "This is a Christian country." The church is not just a collection of beautiful old buildings. It is a living, active force doing great works across our country. Yes, we are a nation that embraces, welcomes, and accepts all faiths and none, but we

are still a Christian country. And as a Christian country, our responsibilities don't end there.

We have a duty to speak out about the persecution of Christians
around the world too."[2]

Great Britain is still a Christian country? I thought they were the ones with
a reputation of boarded-up church buildings, plummeting church attendance,
and an influx of new Muslim immigrants. And yet their Prime Minister made
that bold declaration? How can that be?

I suppose none of us know for sure why Prime Minister Cameron chose to
make that public statement, but we can surmise he thought it an important
thing for his nation to declare. So if Great Britain is a Christian nation, what
does that say about us? Would our leaders call the United States of America a
Christian nation?

Demographic polls of our nation reveal that 70 percent of Americans still
list Christian as their religious preference. Other groups are tiny in comparison
including 3 percent atheist, 2 percent Jewish, and less than 1 percent Muslim.
But even though the majority of Americans are Christian, that does not answer
our question at hand.[3]

Is America a Christian nation or not?

If you want to have an interesting afternoon try googling the question,
"Is America a Christian nation?" All kinds of answers—and angry discussion
boards—will immediately pop up on your computer screen. Fasten your seat
belts. In this section, we will consider the wide range of answers we would find
to this important question.

Question: Is America a Christian Nation?

Possible answer(s): Check all that apply.

- ☐ We are a Christian nation because of the faith of the founders.
- ☐ We are a Christian nation because the principles of our government were borrowed from the Bible and Judeo-Christian[4] principles.

☐ We are a Christian nation, but our founders did not want one official brand of Christianity to be imposed so they enacted freedom
of religion.

☐ We are a Christian nation because of the dedication of this nation
to the Lord by the founders.

☐ We are called by God to be a Christian nation and to be a light to
the world.

☐ We are a Christian nation, but we are not acting like it right now.

Ok, that is a reasonable list for the affirmative crowd. But keep reading. We
have many more possible answers to consider even though this list is getting
long.

■ We were never a Christian nation because the founders were not
really Christians.

■ We were never a Christian nation because the founders were smart
and said all religions are equal therefore we will have no central
religious belief.

■ We were never a Christian nation because there is no such thing as
a Christian nation.

■ We were a fake Christian nation because no real Christian nation
could have been "imperialists" or enslaved the black man.

This is a ridiculous number of options, but that is exactly the point.

■ We were a Christian nation, but now we are not.

■ We were a Christian nation and since the modern polls still say
Christians are the largest self-identified religious group, we are still
one today.

■ We were a Christian nation, but since the Christians in this nation
have moved away from traditional Christian beliefs, we are no
longer a Christian nation.

■ We were a Christian nation, but we aren't now because the government is making decisions that violate God's laws.

- We were a Christian nation, but Christians withdrew from government and failed to hold the ground.

Is your heading spinning? This is why this question in the airwaves around us is so o-v-e-r-w-h-e-l-m-i-n-g. Now for three more that really scramble the options....

- Of course we are not. "America as Christian" is a concept only reserved for God's nation, Israel.
- Whether we were or not is immaterial because God is sovereign over the destinies of all nations, and in the end times America will not stand.
- We should not even be asking this question because the church should only be talking about the Kingdom of God not the nations of man.

Is that not outlandish? How can there be so many options to a seemingly simple question? And those are just the possibilities offered by people who claim a Christian viewpoint. Never mind what the secularists, postmodernists, Muslims, or atheists have to say about the issue. It is no wonder the average American Christian feels so overwhelmed with the "Christian nation" discussion. The deeper I researched, the more major discrepancies I found on this question among our Christian leaders. And it wasn't just among leaders who I would have labeled as post-Christian themselves. I am talking about those who, on main issues, seem to be holding firm to their Biblical values.

There is no universally recognized rules for defining the phrase "Christian nation" let alone a central answer as to whether we were one or are one today. That is why the variation of response is stunning.

I was alarmed, to put it mildly! If we, in the church, cannot agree on what has happened to us in our own nation, how will we ever move forward when we are under pressure of the dark flood? Because of our conflicting views, we could just sit around in the body of Christ arguing in circles to the point where we end up destroying each another.

Hmmm. Could it just be that is exactly what some want us to do? Self-destruct. Does our splintered confusion actually advance the cause of those who want Christian values banished from this nation? Before we go any further in this discussion to figure out whether we are a Christian nation, perhaps we had better realize something foundational for our discussion.

The Rules Have Changed … Dramatically

We are living in a world where the rules have changed.

All kinds of rules have changed, and that is a prominent feature of the dark flood we are learning about.

Up is down, and down is up. Right is wrong, and wrong is right. Good is bad, and bad is good.

At least that is what we have been told by those who changed the rules.

And now, sometimes without us even realizing it, we are tempted to decide things differently because we live in a world following these new rules. Without me explaining myself further, do you already intuitively know what I mean? Following are some of the "new rules" I have noticed. See if you think I am right.

The New Rules in America We Are Supposed to Believe

- Man is improving.
- Rules are restrictive.
- Judging is bad.
- Science is truth.
- Truth is emerging.
- Peace is possible.
- Religions are equal.
- Open-minded is good.
- Competition is bad.
- Borders are porous.
- Capitalism is evil.
- Money is wicked.

- America is suspect.
- All are entitled.
- Morals are relative.
- Politically-correct is necessary.
- Laws are bad.
- Tolerance is love.
- History is changing.
- God is questionable.
- People are good.

What else would you add to my list?

We can debate when these new ideas came into effect and how they came into power, but I do not think there is much debate left that somehow these are the new rules for our society. These are the rules even for those of us who don't like them or think them true.

Now go back and read that list again. S-l-o-w-l-y. Please consider how much these new rules could be messing us up. Even if we partly believed them and interspersed them around the old rules, they would fundamentally change our world.

These new ideas have intruded our homes, invaded our businesses, and set the agenda for our national government. Most of us don't like to talk about them because they are "messy" and provoke conflict, so we learn to "go along with the rules" to avoid social consequences.

As I was exploring how to explain this, I ran across an article written by Peggy Noonan, former speech writer for President Reagan and conservative columnist for *The Wall Street Journal*. Noonan's poignant writing explained eloquently what I was struggling to put into words about the new rules:

> This is for me the moment when the new America began: I was at a graduation ceremony at a public high school in New Jersey. It was 1971 or 1972. One by one a stream of black-robed students walked across the stage and received their diplomas. And a pretty young girl with red hair, big under her graduation gown, walked up to receive hers. The auditorium stood up and applauded. I looked at my sister: "She's going to have a baby." The girl was eight months pregnant and had had the

courage to go through with her pregnancy and take her finals and finish school despite society's disapproval.

But society wasn't disapproving. It was applauding. Applause is a right and generous response for a young girl with grit and heart. And yet, in the sound of that applause I heard a wall falling, a thousand-year wall, a wall of sanctions that said: We as a society do not approve of teen-age unwed motherhood because it is not good for the child, not good for the mother, and not good for us.

The old America had a delicate sense of the difference between the general "we disapprove" and the particular "let's go help her." We had the moral self-confidence to sustain the paradox, to sustain the distance between "official" disapproval and "unofficial" succor. The old America would not have applauded the girl in the big graduation gown; some of its individuals would have helped her not only materially but also with some measure of emotional support. We don't so much anymore. For all our tolerance and talk we don't show much love to what used to be called "girls in trouble." As we've gotten more open-minded we've gotten more closed-hearted."[5]

As soon as I read this, I could hear the new rules screaming at me in my mind. "Oh no, that is a mean story!" I thought. A poor pregnant girl needs total acceptance and applause. Peggy Noonan, you are so wrong!

Then I thought again about the change Noonan was reporting, and in another instant I knew she was right. Way back in 1971 something difficult to describe did change. "The old America" she was describing did die, and the new America rose to take its place. It was subtle, yet massive. Elusive, yet obvious to spot.

If you are not sure this is right, go ask a person in their eighties to share with you his or her perspective. What happened back then opened the floodgate on our world today.

Another Set of Rules

Before we leave the "new rules" discussion, we will dig one layer deeper into our problem. We need to talk about a man who wrote his own set of rules that most of us do not know much about. His name was Saul Alinsky, and his book *Rules for Radicals*[6] released in 1971 has made the rounds on conservative talk show circles for years. Perhaps you have heard of him or his book or perhaps, like many Americans, you have not.

Saul Alinsky was a community organizer whose work became the "blueprint" by many who wanted to institute societal change both back then and in recent years. Back in the 1970s *TIME* magazine said, "It is not too much to argue that American democracy is being altered by Alinsky ideas."[7] A quick read of an Alinsky interview with *Playboy* magazine in 1972 would reveal the potential danger of this man's conniving strategies in the hands of activists or political leaders.[8] The reputed effectiveness of his methods coupled with his flippant dedication of his book to Satan should be enough to cause any Christian great alarm.

Alinsky was very clear about the intentions for his strategies in the introduction to his book:

> What follows is for those who want to change the world from what it is to what they believe it should be. *The Prince* was written by Machiavelli for the Haves on how to hold power. *Rules for Radicals* is written for the Have-Nots on how to take it away.[9]

What if activist groups have learned and applied Mr. Alinsky's rules to effectively bring change to our current culture? That is exactly what is being proposed by those who have watched the great flood waters rise in our nation. They say that we, the American people, have been "Alinsky-ized," and most of us don't even recognize it. Both Barack Obama and Hillary Clinton have ties to Alinsky's teachings.[10] The quick rise of the gay agenda and the modern progressive movement is evidence of Alinsky rules in play.

Honestly, I think they are right. I believe public opinion has been, in part, manipulated using techniques that are difficult to recognize and are built on strategic lying and exaggeration. That is, I believe, why so many illogical changes have taken root in our nation so quickly. Here is the idea behind Alinsky's community organization techniques. The goal is to push for change among people by overreaching with an idea. The change agent is to look like they are trying to get some sort of huge thing accomplished. They talk big and intimidate. Then when that huge change is too radical for people to receive yet, they compromise. If the organizer keeps that process up long enough, they will move the boundaries and get the change they desire piece by piece.

In some ways this concept is a cousin to the propaganda technique successfully used by the Nazis called "The Big Lie."[11] The Big Lie theory says people are more likely to believe a big lie than a smaller one because the big lie is so outlandish they assume it would have to be true since anyone dared to say it! Those using the technique will then lie frequently and passionately until the people let go of the old ideologies and adopt the lie.

Below you will find a list of Alinsky's twelve rules from his book. For right now, do not get hung up on trying to understand all of them as they can be tricky without further explanation. Just read them now, and more about how they are used will be explained later in the book.

Rules for Radicals:

Rule 1: Power is not only what you have, but what the enemy thinks you have.

Rule 2: Never go outside the expertise of your people.

Rule 3: Whenever possible, go outside the expertise of the enemy.

Rule 4: Make the enemy live up to his own book of rules.

Rule 5: Ridicule is man's most potent weapon.

Rule 6: A good tactic is one your people enjoy.

Rule 7: A tactic that drags on too long becomes a drag.

Rule 8: Keep the pressure on. Never let up.

Rule 9: The threat is usually more terrifying than the thing itself.

Rule 10: If you push a negative hard enough, it will push through and become positive.

Rule 11: The price of a successful attack is a constructive alternative.

Rule 12: Pick the target, freeze it, personalize it, and polarize it.[12]

Can you see evidence of any of these techniques being used in public places today? I certainly can. Here are two examples that come to mind. Example one is Planned Parenthood. Even after the Center for Medical Progress videos[13] revealed the lies and deceptions surrounding the abortion practices in Planned Parenthood, the barbarism was still defended by politicians, the Planned Parenthood officials continued to lie, conservatives were painted as women haters, and the funding of Planned Parenthood was supported by a majority of Americans. How crazy!

Example two is Bruce Jenner.[14] We were told very loudly that he was undergoing a normalizing procedure. How did we get to the place where the American public would not only accept the Jenner narrative but even call him an American hero for his choices?

On September 15, 2015, President Obama issued an executive order titled "Using Behavioral Science Insights to Better Serve the American People." This initiative directs the Social and Behavioral Science Team (SBCT) to provide agencies help on how to structure choices to the American public.[15] *Forbes* magazine labels this the "White House's 'nudge' unit"[16] based on the best-selling book by the title of *Nudge*.[17] The question becomes: "Who is doing the nudging, and what are they nudging us toward?" Why does the executive branch feel the need to help us structure our choices?

Now lest we think that manipulation is only used in the political world, I would suggest we should look more closely. These tactics can be common in the schoolyard, the living room, or even in the church boardroom. Basically any place where man's flesh is set loose, his selfish motives and his evil desires are allowed to manipulate.

So let's get back to the premise of why we just talked about the Alinsky list. Here is our summary: The rules have changed. The flood has invaded. And we are living in a nation that has experienced rapid fundamental change.

We, as Christians, want answers. We want to find where our problem is and fix it right away. But it is just not that easy. Tricky forces of darkness have deceived the masses and neutralized voices of reason. Many good, well-meaning people have believed the false narrative. We, as followers of Christ, are struggling to stay grounded and sort out the truth from the error.

We take our best stab at figuring out what to do in this hour knowing by very design we have a problem. We want to make a Godly response. But we are flooded with opinions, and we have two very real handicaps clouding our perceptions. First is the list of new rules that have infiltrated our minds and confused our views. Second are these manipulation techniques that have been used to advance the dark flood cause.

Rather creepy, huh? To think we could have been collectively indoctrinated! But if we have, it is time for us to recognize it, and it is time we quit cooperating with Satan's plan to neutralize, discredit, and destroy not only our nation but also our fellow Christians.

Pulling This Together to Get An Answer

So we have successfully identified three things on the way to answering our original question in this chapter, that of "Is America a Christian Nation?" There are at least eighteen possible responses to that question among Christians. The rules in America have changed, and these "new rules" may affect how we answer such questions. We may have been unduly manipulated into the "new rules" by dark manipulative techniques.

Given all the obstacles, it is challenging to make determinations. We could decide not to answer our question, but not deciding what is happening here is not going to help us walk into our future. It is disorienting and weak to not know who you were…or who you are called to be!

So here is what I suggest we do. Let's focus on what I believe most Christians can agree on. I would call these the "minimal facts" about our nation. See what you think of my list.

10 Things We Can (Minimally) Determine About America As a "Christian Nation"

1. The founders were (at the very least) God-fearing people who chose to use "God words" in the founding documents. For example, "Creator" was used in the Declaration of Independence.[18]

2. The law and morality in our government was based on Judeo-Christian traditions. (Ex. Our legal system is based on truth-telling unlike Islamic law, which permits forms of lying.[19] We used the biblical standards of absolute truth as the basis of our criminal law.)

3. Presidents and leaders of our nation have historically invoked the blessing of God over our nation in prayer, and their definition of God was the Christian God, beginning with George Washington and many others.[20]

4. Our national buildings and monuments in Washington, DC display massive amount of Christian influence in art and historical documents. (A tour of DC will confirm this.)[21]

5. The Ten Commandments were taught in our American school systems until the mid-1960s.[22]

6. The overwhelmingly largest religious segment of our nation throughout its entire history has been Christianity.[23]

7. We have never been known to the world as a "Muslim nation."

8. Historically, we have had a reputation among the nations of being a "Christian nation" at least because that has been the dominant religion of our citizens.

9. The Western Judeo-Christian value system has traditionally been intertwined within our American culture. For example, until

recently we celebrated Christian holidays, such as Christmas, as a culture.

10. The Christian church of America for most of our history has been credited with positive social influence, such as Christian-run hospitals, social service agencies, military chaplaincies and the like.

If you notice, I used a conservative approach to all ten evaluations above to form the basis for my conclusion.

Yes, I believe we, in the past, have been a "Christian nation" based on the minimum definition above. I believe the evidence (which is beyond the scope of this book) is conclusive and worth further study. But no, I do not believe we are currently a "Christian nation." For, in all kinds of ways that define us as a nation, we have slipped into something different. We are now "post-Christian."

We are a nation with many sincere Christians. We are a nation with many people who are praying to God through Jesus Christ. We are a nation in which the Church of Jesus Christ is very much alive and praying for our country. But in our official national identity of collective life together, we have changed. We are not holding to a traditional Judeo-Christian system.

We are multicultural...but we are no longer a melting pot of one dominant culture.

We are secular.

We are God-less.

We are post-Christian.

And that is why *Obergefell v. Hodges* was able to happen.

This diagnosis is supported by two major pieces of information. First, an overwhelming majority of Americans see themselves as a land of religious diversity. Since we are a democratic republic, this is significant. In a July 2015 survey of American citizens, only 19 percent believe we are a Christian nation, while 69 percent believe we are a nation of many religions, and 9 percent claim we are a secular nation. "Debate about whether America is a Christian nation will continue," Scott McConnell of Lifeway Research said. "Although most Americans are Christians, they understand a nation founded on principles of religious freedom will be a nation of many faiths."[24]

That brings me to evidence number two as to why we are no longer a Christian nation. It is based on what President Obama declared in 2007 when he was running for President that he later reiterated once in office.

> Whatever we once were, we're no longer just a Christian nation; we are also a Jewish nation, a Muslim nation, a Buddhist nation, a Hindu nation, and a nation of nonbelievers.[25]

I guess President Obama, like David Cameron, wanted the world—and us—to know: the rules have changed.

And that pretty much sums it up for now. How we respond to that news will, in many ways, determine what happens to our future. Let's check out in chapter four how many of us are choosing to respond.

CHAPTER 4

EXILED IN OUR OWN NATION

One can certainly understand the joy that LGBT Americans and their supporters feel today. But orthodox Christians must understand that things are going to get much more difficult for us. We are going to have to learn how to live as exiles in our own country. We are going to have to learn how to live with at least a mild form of persecution. And we are going to have to change the way we practice our faith and teach it to our children to build resilient communities.[1]

—Rod Dreher

Something has died. It has not just changed, it has died. The problem is, it is hard to figure out exactly what expired. I suppose each of us could describe it differently. But as I listen to the hearts of those who love Jesus and our concern about this dark flood, I can hear the same sentiment expressed a variety of ways.

Something has died. And we do not like it. In fact, we hate it and all that it represents.

If someone were to ask you "what died in America?," which of these would you consider as true:

- ☐   our Christian identity in America
- ☐   our way of life
- ☐   our sense of religious freedom
- ☐   our pride in our nation
- ☐   our sense of stability
- ☐   our moral and ethical standards
- ☐   our dream for the future
- ☐   the futures for our children
- ☐   our marriage definition
- ☐   our innocence
- ☐   our Judeo-Christian values
- ☐   our churches
- ☐   our foundation of truth
- ☐   our children's faith in Jesus
- ☐   our children's holy standards
- ☐   our Constitution
- ☐   our trust in government

Did you note more than one as what you are feeling? No wonder we are so upset!

While I was working on this section of the book I got an urgent Facebook message from a friend. She is a hero of mine. As a young millennial she serves the Lord faithfully and is raising young children to do the same. Her tone was both urgent and tragic. She had been sobbing for twenty-five minutes before contacting me, she said.

It seems that a middle-aged family friend in her community—the father of kids she grew up with and a pastor at a local church—had just been arrested on charges of sexual assault of a minor boy. The last line of her message pierced me, "Lisa, it just breaks my heart this is hitting so close to home. I feel like I am in mourning. This is all just unfolding, and it is very hard to even believe." You see my friend had experienced death. Something died for her that day. A relationship. A trust. A piece of her innocence. A belief in the sanctity of pastors' lives. The dark flood had invaded her personal space, and she was left figuring out how to respond.

I believe, as followers of Jesus Christ worldwide but especially as the church of the United States of America, we are suffering what this young women identified. We are in grief. We are in a state of shock. We are traumatized. And now we are in collective mourning.

As the rapid shifts have hit our land, and as the old rules have been buried under the new rules of our land, it feels to us as if something beautiful has died. We want to talk about it, but, as in most forms of grief, our feelings and our thoughts are odd, jumbled, and uncomfortable.

We don't want to be labeled as old fashioned and backward as if our talk of the "good old days" made us see the past with rose-colored glasses. But we earnestly want to express our pain somehow as the daily news feels more like an obituary to an old way of life than an exciting bridge to our future.

Some of us remember when children's sports leagues were not played on Sunday morning and when schools all had Christmas programs instead of holiday sings. Some of us had granddads who were respected in the community as "preachers" who hung out at the public school by day to pray with the kids and then went to church at night for the revival meeting. We remember when homosexuality was labeled a problem and pornography was hidden in a bag.

If we talk about these things, we risk being dismissed as naïve and outdated, like relics of a past era who need to retire. But we are not naïve. We are a people mourning. We don't like it that our own fond memories are tarnished by televangelist scandals and sports heroes who at retirement age decide to change their gender. We feel duped and damaged, hollow and angry. But most of all we are very sad because something has died.

Call it our trust in human decency, or our belief in an unspoken moral code, or whatever you want, but, bless our little hearts, we are disappointed, and you won't talk us out of the feeling that something has died!

Southern Baptist leader Russell Moore wrote,

> The idea of America as "post-Christian" then calls the church to a sort of freaked-out nostalgia. We identify our focal point in some made-up past—whether the founding era, or the 1950s or the 1980s or whenever.

That makes us all the more frantic when we see the moral chaos around us. We see it in terms of "moral decline" instead of seeing it the way the Bible does, in terms of not decline but of Fall.[2]

I get what he is saying to an extent. And I think he is right about us needing a reality check about the Fall, but I think he might be missing an intangible reality here. Mr. Moore, you cannot talk people out of their grief if they believe something has died. (We have learned that in working with families who have lost a loved one.)

Has anyone in your family died? It is a very painful and personal ordeal. Each family member has their own grief response as they struggle to recover from their shock and make peace with their new reality of loss. Thoughts and feelings are sometimes unreasonable. Family members must give room to each other if healing and new life is to be restored.

This brings me to the question of this chapter. What would happen to a people group if they collectively experienced loss of their heritage and their identity? Would it not cause a grief response? Jeremiah describes collective grief in his nation when they fell into in the face of captivity.

> Judah mourns, and her gates languish; her people lament on the ground, and the cry of Jerusalem goes up.
>
> —JEREMIAH 14:2, ESV

We know the face of national mourning on a large scale when something tragic happens in our land. Presidential assassinations and the planes crashing into the twin towers are the big moments that mark our minds. But what about the seasons of death that enter our world slowly—like a long terminal dying process where a loved one gradually slips away? Is it possible these death experiences displace us more than we even imagine? That grief-filled place is what Rod Dreher talks about when he proposes that Christians are now in exile in our nation.[3]

Our Grief Response

Grief is tricky to resolve but remarkably understandable. Elizabeth Kubler Ross in her 1969 book *On Death and Dying* teaches that grief has five predictable stages. We usually apply these stages to individuals, but these stages could also explain some of the unusual reactions we are observing among our fellow Christians. Let's take a look.

The Five Stages of Grief

1. Denial—The first reaction is denial. In this stage individuals believe the diagnosis is somehow mistaken, and cling to a false, preferable reality.

2. Anger—When the individual recognizes that denial cannot continue, he becomes frustrated, especially at proximate individuals. Certain responses of a person undergoing this phase would be: "Why me? It's not fair!" "How can this happen to me?" "Who is to blame?" "Why would this happen?"

3. Bargaining—The third stage involves the hope that the individual can avoid a cause of grief. Usually, the negotiation for an extended life is made in exchange for a reformed lifestyle. People facing less serious trauma can bargain or seek compromise.

4. Depression—"I'm so sad, why bother with anything?" "I'm going to die soon, so what's the point?" "I miss my loved one, why go on?" During the fourth stage, the individual becomes saddened by the mathematical probability of death. In this state, the individual may become silent, refuse visitors, and spend much of the time mournful and sullen.

5. Acceptance—"It's going to be okay." "I can't fight it; I may as well prepare for it." "Nothing is impossible." In this last stage, individuals embrace mortality or the inevitable future, or that of a loved one or other tragic event.[4]

I believe these five stages could help explain the many responses we see today among those of us who believe in the reality of the dark flood. Let's go through each step and see how we might apply it to the church in America today.

Denial

Sometimes we hear full-blown denial in action, and sometimes it is more like an unusual hybrid form. People say things like:

- "Yeah, things were tough when I was growing up too, but everything just seemed to eventually work out all right."
- "I don't think all those problems like homosexuality and other sexual immoralities really happen in our community. We are in the Bible belt." (I have heard this so many times from so many locations around the nation, I am seriously wondering...how big is this belt?)
- "We keep our kids pretty protected around here. I've heard about how young people all over the nation are falling away from the Bible, but our kids seem to have their heads on straight." (This one is always said in the adult meetings while the teens sit sheepishly quiet in the back pew of the church.)
- "The USA has always been the strongest nation."
- "We were chosen by God to do a great work."
- "We will never fall. Our military is too strong!" (This one is usually accompanied by random patriotic trinketry displayed on the lapel or back bumper of the car.)

Did you recognize those voices of denial? Let's look the second stage.

Anger

I hear it seeping out of American Christians who are beginning to recognize their loss with words such as:

- "Whose fault is this anyway?"
- "How did we get in this mess?"
- "Why, if those pastors had been preaching the true word of God like they were back in my day, most of this foolishness would be gone before it ever got started!"

- "I think it is the men's fault. Absentee fathers are ruining the land."
- "Well, I think it is the women's fault. If they had not pushed for equal rights, we would not see this level of destruction in the nation."
- "I am sure it's the Democratic machinery. Their crazy liberal policies have destroyed the land and infiltrated the church!"
- "Well, I'm sure it is the Republican machinery. They were greedy, and look what that has done!"
- "It's these young millennials!"
- "No, it's these backslidden lazy baby boomers!"

And the blame game goes on and on. Sometimes the accusations are true, but the issues are never worked on because they are fueled by the drama of the flood and distorted by our collective grief. That brings us to stage number three.

Bargaining

This is where we try to negotiate or seek compromise to avoid the reality of death. Boy, do we have a significant case of this going on in the church right now while we try to keep the peace and avoid anymore bleed from church attendance, especially in the young generation.

- "Our church just chooses not to speak publicly about those tough controversial issues that are dividing the nation. We just preach Jesus."
- "Millennials say they are offended by the church's traditional narrow definitions of sexual morality. So we went back and looked at those scriptures and found out all this time—why for over 2,000 years—the church has been misinterpreting!"
- "Hey, if they will keep coming to church we will be happy to dump the hymnals and crank up the electric guitars!"
- "We will get a younger pastor. We must keep pace, you know."

And the bargaining list goes on and on until some hit the fourth stage.

Depression

We might need to rename this one due to the derogatory nature of that word. We in the church are not depressed. We are just very, very discouraged. I hear it from one end of the nation to the other. My conversation goes something like this when I greet people I have not seen in a while:

- "Hey, so good to see you! How are you and your group doing?"
- "Well Lisa, it has been a tough year. Honestly, we are pretty discouraged," they say with heads hanging low.

It happened so often last year that I began to expect it as the common response!

Now please do not think I am poking fun at these evidences of grief breaking out all around us. Grief is very real, and is to be respected as definitely no fun. As we take note of our collective state, we want to be part of the solution instead of more of the problem. Grief counselors agree that the stages of grief must be lived instead of skipped or ignored as if they are optional.

So that leads me to the fifth and final stage.

Acceptance

This is where we are ready to say something like: We are no longer a Christian nation. If that seems too dramatic, we at least can recognize large portions of our national collective Judeo-Christian standards have died.

Realistic assessment mixes with healthy adjustment, and we are now free to move on to the new reality of our circumstances. What will it take for us to get to this stage even when we do not like the reality of the death?

I thought of four things that might help us move the healing along.

1.   First, we need to acknowledge the grief process. Giving ourselves permission to face this loss situation will allow us to move forward.

2.   Second, we need to allow our fellow Christians some room to resolve this grief under the leadership of the Lord. Their response

could be messy. Some may be stuck in one of the stages in a way that we do not think is appropriate. Prayer and patience will be more helpful than criticism. Talking about the grief process with those whom you are closest is a healthy way to open communication lines between people and share deeper concerns and fears.

3. Third, we must guard ourselves from making poor decisions when we are being unduly influenced by our own experience of grief. Do not make doctrinal or policy statements when grief emotions are leading rather than the Holy Spirit.

4. And fourth, we need to petition the Lord for His healing of our hearts and our land. The body of Christ needs encouraging like never before.

Brothers and sisters, we have lost something. At least for now. And maybe for as long as we live. Many of our dreams are dead. But remember: death is not our final answer! Our citizenship is not here, but eternal, and our hope knows no bounds.

So mourn...but not as the world does, for we are a people of life. God has our future securely in His hands. He is not finished with America or the church yet! Remember weeping may last for a night, but joy comes in the morning! He is personally in this battle with us beckoning us forward in hope no matter what comes knocking on our door.

CHAPTER 5

WHEN THE FLOOD HITS OUR FRONT DOOR

Love does not delight in evil but rejoices with the truth.

—1 Corinthians 13:6

The girl's parents got the invitation for their daughter to take the babysitting job while they were visiting in the neighbor's driveway. The neighbors were a young couple with a new baby that needed an occasional teenage sitter. The couple would pay quite well, and the home was close by so their teen daughter would be able to work without needing transportation. There was just one problem with the plan. The young couple was not married. And, for all appearances from the outside, they had no intention of tying the knot. The parents of the teen were in a quandary of what to do. They really wanted to reach out to this young couple who needed to hear about Jesus. In fact, they had been doing their best to shower this family with unconditional love. But they were getting concerned that their efforts may have backfired in some ways. Now their teenage daughter was acting like the cohabitation arrangement next door was just no big deal. The parents were hesitant to let their daughter be employed and risk a further normalization of the couple's family decisions. But they also did not want to risk the angry separation from both their daughter and the young couple if they said no.

The flood had hit the neighborhood's front door.

The young girl had been a regular in our church program for a number of years. Her parents were not coming with her to worship services but the evidence of growth in her own fourteen-year-old life was apparent. That is why the church leaders were so sad to discover that she was pregnant by another fellow eighth grader who had also been coming to church. The response they made was quick and sure. They supported her firm conviction to bear this young life. But they were not prepared for the stir her pregnancy would cause among the other young girls in the church. She, unlike previous generations who might have been shunned for her pregnant state, was now the new, cool, teen mom. In fact, she was so cool we were concerned she would start a new trend among our kids who had grown up with the *16 and Pregnant Reality Show*. What could they do to uphold biblical standards of holiness and also a pro-life stance?

The flood had hit the church's front door.

The young couple stood quietly in line to talk with me at the end of our session. They nervously began their narrative by telling me of how much they loved their own children ages six and eight. But they were also quick to explain how much they loved their extended family. Their parents. Their siblings. All the people they both held dear. Here was their dilemma. They did not know what to do with their Christmas invitation. It seemed the wife's brother had recently come out of the closet as gay and, while the news was extremely distressing to his parents who were Christians, the wife's mother was insisting that no new arrangements should be made for the annual family get-together. The mother did not know why their daughter was uncomfortable bringing her two young children to the gay couple's home for the traditional overnight celebration. Pain and conflict had resulted, and the couple wanted to hear my opinion on what to do.

The flood had hit the couple's front door.

The pastor had been a faithful minister of the gospel for more than twenty-five years. His commitment to the Lord was unwavering, and his passion for the Lord was unchallenged. That is why his recent announcement of his doctrinal shift came as such a surprise to his congregation. He no longer believed homosexuality was a sin. He was now ready to embrace the possibility that gay marriage was a long overlooked option in the Christian faith. As those closest to him struggled to understand his flip-flopped position, his next announcement cleared up their confusion. The pastor's son had just announced his identification as gay.

The flood had hit the pastor's front door.

The young college student had been a leader among his church's youth program. His testimony had been an inspiration to his group of high school peers. That is why his first holiday home from college was such a disappointment. The liberal views of the professors and the party life at the fraternity had become this man's new life. He was having trouble understanding why his youth pastor and his parents were so upset.

The flood had hit the college dorm.

The new youth pastor was looking for some wise advice. He was obviously very committed to the young lives he had been entrusted to disciple, yet he had a hit a snag. It seems that a teenage boy in his group was struggling with his sexual identity. In fact, the boy was so convinced he was a she that he had begun to dress as a woman and had taken on a new feminine name. The other parents in the youth group were questioning what the youth pastor would say and do. He loved this young man and wanted nothing less than the best for his life. He felt it would be wrong to push the confused young student away from the church youth group, yet he could certainly appreciate the concern of the other parents who did not want this young man's behaviors and beliefs to spread to their young Christian children.

The flood had hit the youth room's front door.

The employee had proven himself as valuable. So valuable that customers often asked for him specifically by name. Joe's bright energetic personality was as contagious as his loving smile that seemed to melt away tension and conflict. He was always ready to pray for anyone who had need or was going through a tough time. That's why Joe's wife's visit came as such a shock. Joe was addicted to pornography? And he used the office computer to log in every day? It must be some kind of sick joke!

The flood had hit the business's front door.

It is not that hard to talk about this "great flood of evil" if we are just railing about the policies in Washington and the laws that have changed "out there." But we are not just looking on from afar. Not anymore.

Several years ago maybe we could have a hypothetical philosophical discussion about such issues as gender identity, homosexuality, teen pregnancy, pornography, or cohabitation. Now, our flood discussions are far more personal. They have names and faces attached to them as well as a host of confusing emotions.

You see, what is often driving the force of the flood is no longer some activist who is trying to get his or her way. It is us. Our friends and our families. Those whom we love have fallen into the flood, and we have felt the pressure and changed.

Researcher David Walker, when reporting about the radical shifting in our nation concerning the support of gay marriage stated, "It is not just marriage that has changed." The findings, he explained, are a result of changing attitudes about the gay, lesbian, bisexual, and transgender community as a whole. He believes this level of acceptance was unimaginable a few years ago.

"What is really driving this [change] is knowing gay people," Walker said. He said personal contact with gay family members, gay friends, and gay neighbors is winning what activists call the battle for 'hearts and minds.'"[1]

How can we get upset with family members and friends who find themselves in these very delicate situations? How can we say "no" to the lifestyle of a person when we know it could cost us the relationships that we hold dear? How can we not listen to the distress cries of those who say the church has misunderstood and ignored their needs?

These are the heartbreaking questions that the flood brings to our front door. Personal questions. Personal pressures that are not easily dismissed as political ideology, doctrinal discussion, or philosophical muse.

I am in no way going to minimize the complexity of these questions or offer glib, insensitive responses to those whom these issues are immensely personal. This is a pain-filled flood. Millions are weeping in its wake. It is devastating to the very inner points of our human relationships.

There was a time in our own family's life that I was extremely tempted to make a "relationship saving" adjustment because of the dark flood. It happened several years ago when our then 15-year-old daughter had fallen deeply into distress after being lured into a secret abusive relationship with a 46-year-old man from our church. Kalyn, in the midst of her wounds and pain, became deceived and isolated from the God who wanted to heal her heart. I watched helplessly while her life spun out of control. She did not want to face the complexity of her wounds at that time. She wanted her parents and her family to pretend that the problems we saw in her life were not problems at all. She wanted us to rewrite our understanding of holiness to allow for some of her dysfunctional coping methods.

She was very angry at us because she was so miserable in her secret world of pain. I would have done most anything to help her get healed and happy again. And on many occasions, I was even incredibly tempted! I wanted my daughter's heart back so badly it seemed halfway reasonable to my mother's heart to do whatever it took to bring her heart home. Even if that meant I had to "soften doctrines" or "move the truth" to get the job done.

But here is what my daughter said about that idea after her multi-year recovery from her pain:

> I was immensely trapped in my own world of pain and did not think there was a way out. I was very angry and determined to work out my pain on my own terms by running to other guys to feel loved. I remember being furious that my parents were not willing to let me stay in my place of deception. I would yell at them and try to make them just leave me alone, but deep down, I was desperate for someone to say no to my dysfunctional mess.
>
> I am so grateful my parents did not bow to my pressure! Their courage to tell me "no" saved my life. They never stopped loving me, but they also refused to compromise the truth. I would not be happily married with beautiful children of my own if they had given in and let the devil win. It is absolutely necessary to tell a person trapped in darkness about their sin. It might be painful, and they will likely bristle. But in the end, they will thank you.

(To read more about our daughter's struggle and her ultimate healing or to get help in your family if you are facing any type of dark and confusing situations of pain, get a copy of our book *Unmask the Predators*. In that resource we outline a prayer strategy that has brought wisdom and support to many who faced overwhelming circumstances and challenges of darkness.)

At the base of this issue is this: Truth cannot be revised if it is real truth. And truth, no matter what the modern activists or wounded victims may say, is only discernible through the accurate lens of God's Word. Period.

Truth embraced is what finally set our daughter free. And it was our best—yet most painful—act of kindness we have ever performed to love her truthfully.

Michael Brown in his book *Can You Be Gay and Christian?* states, "While it is true that many 'gay Christians' have been wounded by the church, and while the church has often failed miserably in reaching out with compassion to LGBT people, the greatest possible expression of love is to tell people God's truth, knowing that His ways are best."[2]

So love equals telling the truth, in God's timing and in His way.

We see these concepts of truth and love linked together in Scripture perfectly in 1 Corinthians 13:4–6:

> Love is patient. Love is kind. . . . It does not boast, it is not proud. It is not rude, it is not self-seeking, it is not easily angered, it keeps no record of wrongs. Love does not delight in evil but rejoices with the truth.
>
> —NIV 1984

Becoming a radical truth teller in the face of the flood takes courage . . . and spiritual preparation. It will not come naturally to the human soul. It is costly and will take a faith that is stronger than what many of us are prepared right now to display.

So here is my closing question for this chapter. What will you do when (not if) the flood hits your front door? God is ready to pour out a confident love through us that speaks the truth kindly without pride or anger. We may feel the pressure to compromise, but God is going to strengthen us with faith and power if we continue to radically embrace truth, which leads us to Chapter Six.

CHAPTER 6

WHY *COEXIST* WILL NOT WORK

...what fellowship can light have with darkness?

—2 Corinthians 6:14

It was the year 2001 when a Polish graphic designer won an art contest sponsored by a "socio-political art museum"[1] in Jerusalem. His winning art design was of the word *coexist* featuring three different symbols representing three world's religions and philosophies. The design was later elaborated upon to include eight symbols. Perhaps you are familiar with its look. Driving down my community's side street any day of the week, I can see cars with bumpers displaying this man's coexist design.

The Polish man's design was popular, but the coexist emblem became more popular several years later when Bono, the lead singer from the popular United Kingdom rock band U2, wrote a similar design on a white band and placed it on his forehead while performing at a concert. Bono's fans went crazy as he pointed to the religious icons on his head: the crescent (C) for Islam, the star of David (X) for Judaism, and the cross (T) for Christianity. As the emotion packed stage show progressed, Bono declared: "Jesus, Jews, Muhammad, it's true....All sons of Abraham. Father Abraham, speak to your sons, Tell them, 'No more!'"[2]

Online marketers loved it.

Behind the bumper stickers is something deep and profound. The product hits a cord within the ideological philosophies of many people worldwide. In fact, some might suggest the coexist art drove the ideologies, while others might propose the coexist ideologies drove the art. Either way, the results are worth noting.

The concept of coexisting together in a tolerant co-equal sort of way has a multi-decade history. Learning to dwell together in peace was a big rally cry of the hippy and anti-war movements in the 1960s.

After the hippie movement of the '60s failed to produce world peace, the theme continued to be a part of culture in ad campaigns such as Coca-Cola's 1971 television commercial featuring people from multiple cultures holding their bottles of Coke singing, "I'd Like to Teach the World to Sing in Perfect Harmony."[3] They were going for the same warm fuzzy feeling generated by the "It's a Small World"[4] attraction at Disney theme parks. When we, the public, got done viewing these things, we felt like we had actually done something about world peace.

Then there was the bumper sticker campaign for *Visualize World Peace* invented by a Houston woman in the 1980s and then the massive multiculturalism emphasis that followed that. So what do all these "movements" have in common? Just this: a desire for man to live together in harmony and true love coupled with the belief that man can make that goal possible.[5]

These ideologies of manmade peace are not unique to the twentieth century. In fact, the central idea could be seen all the way back in the 1498 classical novel *Utopia*[6] (made famous in recent times by the chick flick movie *Ever After.*[7]) "In that book the central character Hythloda moves to a discussion of Utopian society, portraying a nation based on rational thought, with communal property, great productivity, no rapacious love of gold, no real class distinctions, no poverty, little crime or immoral behavior, religious tolerance, and little inclination to war."[8]

Coexisting is definitely not a fresh idea. It is an ideology or belief system that can be studied throughout history and societal cycles. It splashes across the pages of history freely, but we, as Americans, do not seem to notice or care. (Perhaps that is because we have so shifted our focus toward STEM [Science, Technology, Engineering, and Math] education in recent years that history has been thrown to the sideline as if it does not matter.)[9]

We must look behind the proponents of the coexist ideologies today to gain a better understanding of what they are really saying.

Why *Coexist* Is Incorrect, Partially Correct, and Doomed

All the above analysis leads us to a series of questions. Could the concept of coexist work? Can all the major religions and all the cultures live together in peace? Would man be able to "get it together" where all could be free to believe what they want and yet never have conflict or struggle? If so, could this be the answer to the dark flood problem? The last question is the most important one of all. Is coexist a true or false ideology according to God?

To answer these questions, let's take a look at what the Bible speaks to this issue. We will start after the account of Noah and the flood. In the listing of Noah's descendants who became many nations (i.e. people groups) this verse in Genesis 10:32 says: "From these the nations spread out over the earth after the flood."

Genesis 11:1 goes on to explain the condition of mankind at that time. "Now the whole world had one language and a common speech." So we see that the people were spread out but at this time, they had one common language and speech. It was out of this common or unified bond that the people said to each other:

> Come, let's make bricks and bake them thoroughly...let us build ourselves a city, with a tower that reaches to the heavens, so that we may make a name for ourselves; otherwise we will be scattered over the face of the whole earth.
>
> —GENESIS 11:3–4

It sounds like a sweet image, does it not? People all together in one accord making a big tower to reach the sky. However, God obviously did not see this cooperative effort as a good thing. In fact, He took strong action against it. As the Lord looked at what they were building He said:

> If as one people speaking the same language they have begun to do this, then nothing they plan to do will be impossible for them. Come, let us go down and confuse their language so they will not understand each other.
>
> —Genesis 11:6–7

The place they were building was named Babel, which sounds like the Hebrew word for confused.

> The Lord scattered them over the face of the whole earth.
>
> —Genesis 11:8

I remember as a young Christian thinking that this is surely one of the strangest stories in the Bible. Why would God do such an odd thing? It seemed like such an anti-utopian view. Man was finally getting it right, I would think. Didn't God want the people all singing together and working on a common goal? I remember struggling from my '70s mindset to accept why God did that.

What I failed to understand back then was what God already intimately knew. Sin would not allow man's cooperative goal to truly succeed. Oh, people could build a tower just as they said they would, but their one world system mixed with their fallen man state would make the results disastrous.

It was not until later in my adult years that someone challenged my '70s mindset long enough for me to look at this story from God's point of view. Think back to what event had immediately preceded the great Tower of Babel social experiment. It was the flood—the dreadful season when God brought judgment on the earth because of man's refusal to submit to His rule.

However, the story of the flood was not just about judgment. It is also about mercy. God knew the condition of man's heart. God had witnessed the results without Him. Man's heart had become so wicked that "every inclination of the thoughts of the human heart was only evil all the time" (Gen. 6:5). It was because of His love that God intervened by saving one man and his family on an ark so that He could remove the unrestrainable evil and repopulate the world again. That is why God was so alarmed when He saw the tower construction. He knew that within the fallen, sinful state of man's heart was a propensity for such rampant, damning sin that He would need to take action to save man from himself.

Remember how God said that nothing would be impossible for them if they built the tower together? God knew the power of unbridled humanism—which is the belief that man is the ultimate solution to all things rather than God. They would have built that tower independent of God and then set it up as the central monument to man's success. Father God, in His mercy, stopped their humanistic plans from working.

The *coexist* ideology is a close cousin to the Babel ideology. Man "coming together" with all tribes, tongues, and nations will happen, but not on this side of heaven. All nations will one day worship at His throne (Jer. 3:17; Ps. 86:9). All knees will bow before Jesus the Lord (Phil. 2:10). However, that is not in this dispensation of time but in the one that is to come. Right now men's souls are in the valley of decision (John 8:12) and the nations are in the Psalm 2 scoffing against the Lord. Those seasons will not change until the Lord returns.

However, end times prophecies from the Book of Daniel and the Book of Revelation reveal that before the Day of the Lord the antichrist will function with a one-world power system. This is why Christians are taught to be wary of any human movement that facilitates a coming together of peoples in a *coexist* philosophy and worship system. Our ears should perk up when we see new campaigns like #globalcitizen[10] and new programs through the United Nations called Project 2030.[11] They are counterfeit solutions to world issues that flow from a one-world government ideology. So *coexist* that leads to humanist one-world government/religious systems is false.

For our next clue as to the Lord's will, let's fast forward to the New Testament and see what Jesus had to say on the *coexist* matter. In Matthew we find an interesting proof of how some part of the *coexist* concept could be true. In Matthew 13 Jesus told the parable of the weeds. In that story He compared the Kingdom of Heaven to a field in which a farmer had sown good seed but an enemy to the farmer had also sowed weed seed among the good seed. Both types of plants grew up together and so the farmer's servants inquired as to whether they should attempt to pull up the weeds. They were instructed to leave the plants together until harvest time.

Later, Jesus explained the meaning of this parable to His disciples like this:

> The one who sowed the good seed is the Son of Man. The field is the world, and the good seed stands for the people of the kingdom. The weeds are the people of the evil one, and the enemy who sows them is the devil. The harvest is the end of the age, and the harvesters are angels. As the weeds are pulled up and burned in the fire, so it will be at the end of the age. The Son of Man will send out his angels, and they will weed out of his kingdom everything that causes sin and all who do evil. They will throw them into the blazing furnace, where there will be weeping and gnashing of teeth. Then the righteous will shine like the sun in the kingdom of their Father. Whoever has ears, let them hear.
>
> —MATTHEW 13:37–43

This is interesting. Jesus is saying here that in the world (the field) the good seed and the weeds will coexist. In fact, they will be allowed to coexist until the end of the age when God will separate them at the judgment. So if what we mean by coexist is the concept that people of all faith and non-faith backgrounds will live together, Jesus would agree. It is true that until Jesus comes back and the new season on earth begins, those who are born again and those who are lost will live together. It would not be correct or godly for us to destroy the weeds, but we must allow God to do His judging work at His appointed time.

This form of *coexist* is not what this movement seems to long for, however. They are pushing more for what was demonstrated by the first Muslim prayer service intermingled with a Christian service in the Washington National Cathedral in November, 2014[12] or by the world's first lesbian bishop from Sweden who called for Christian churches to remove crosses from their sanctuaries so Muslims "won't be offended,"[13] or by what Oprah was tapping into in her mini-series *Belief*.[14] They are designing within their concept of *coexist* a tolerance and universalism that says "all ways can be right." This is another way of saying all roads lead to heaven, and man is in charge of the system of the road!

The coexistence doctrine stands opposed to John 14:6 where Jesus clearly states: "I am the way and the truth and the life. No one comes to the Father except through me." Unfortunately this false ideology has been proclaimed from the highest office of our nation.

George W. Bush when speaking to Al Arabiya News in October of 2007 said, "Well, first of all, I believe in an Almighty God, and I believe that all the world, whether they be Muslim, Christian, or any other religion, prays to the same God. That's what I believe. I believe that Islam is a religion that preaches peace."[15]

With all due respect Mr. President, you are totally wrong! Your views come right off the coexist bumper sticker, but they are not grounded in the Word of God. The following scriptures stand opposed to your ideas:

- Deuteronomy 5:6–7
- Deuteronomy 6:3, 13–15
- Isaiah 45:5
- Matthew 7:13–14
- John 14:6
- John 17:3
- Acts 4:12
- Philippians 2:10
- Revelation 19:16

This heresy of "all roads leading to God" is extremely destructive in our generation. Stephen Prothero in his book, *God Is Not One: The Eight Rival Religions That Run the World* writes: "For more than a generation we have followed scholars and sages down the rabbit hole into a fantasy world where all gods are one....In fact this naïve theological groupthink—call it God think—has made the world more dangerous by blinding us to the clash of religions that threaten us worldwide."[16]

Mr. Prothero is correct. The great clash of religions is not about men needing to be "nicer." It is about ideologies that cannot *coexist* as truth. For instance, the word *Islam* means submission to Allah. The Koran does not declare that Muslims are to "coexist" with the "people of the book," who are Christians. They are to bring the world into submission to Allah.

What Utopian-desiring *coexist* people want is something that is only possible through the One who formed the Earth and sent His only Son. They want peace but not the Prince of Peace. They want love but not the One who is love. They want justice but not the Lawgiver. They want unity but not the Body of Christ. They want freedom but not submission to the One who is freedom. And that is why this *coexist* ideology will never work. We can shout it, sing it, chant it, and put it on a bumper sticker, but it will never work this side of heaven.

Conclusion

You did it. You made it through the first six chapters of the book where we thoroughly determined that first, the Dark Flood is powerful and miserable, and second, that our nation is in trouble, and third, that we are grieving over our current state of affairs and grasping for solutions. Are you ready for some good news now? I know I surely am!

In the next section we will find out *for sure* that there is hope, that God is still working His plan today as He has done throughout the ages, and that if we will trust Him, we will find these to be amazingly awesome days to be alive and serving Him.

PART TWO

FLOOD #2:
THE BEAUTIFUL
FLOOD OF HOPE

CHAPTER 7

THE POWERFUL, BEAUTIFUL FLOOD I DID NOT KNOW

Sometimes beauty is found in the most unlikely places. Sometimes hope is born on what would have been labeled defeat. Before we begin this awesome chapter, we are going to consider the stories of four saints of old. As you read of them, be reminded that they are of the crowd in heaven who is cheering us on today.

> When the members of the Sanhedrin heard this, they were furious and gnashed their teeth at him. But Stephen, full of the Holy Spirit, looked up to heaven and saw the glory of God, and Jesus standing at the right hand of God. "Look," he said, "I see heaven open and the Son of Man standing at the right hand of God." At this they covered their ears and, yelling at the top of their voices, they all rushed at him, dragged him out of the city and began to stone him. Meanwhile, the witnesses laid their coats at the feet of a young man named Saul. While they were stoning him, Stephen prayed, "Lord Jesus, receive my spirit." Then he fell on his knees and cried out, "Lord, do not hold this sin against them." When he had said this he fell asleep.
>
> —STEPHEN, THE FIRST CHRISTIAN MARTYR
> ACTS 7:54–60

But before the wood was set on fire, Ludovicus, duke of Bavaria, with another gentleman with him, which was the son of Clement, came and exhorted John Huss, that he would yet be mindful of his safeguard, and renounce his errors. To whom he said, "What error should I renounce, when I know myself guilty of none? For as for those things which are falsely alleged against me, I know that I never did so much as once think them, much less preach them. For this was the principal end and purpose of my doctrine, that I might teach all men penance and remission of sins, according to the verity of the gospel of Jesus Christ, and the exposition of the holy doctors; wherefore with a cheerful mind and courage I am here ready to suffer death." When he had spoken these words, they left him, and shaking hands together, they departed. Then was the fire kindled, and John Huss began to sing with a loud voice, "Jesus Christ, the Son of the living God, have mercy upon me." And when he began to say the same the third time, the wind drove the flame so upon his face, that it choked him.

—JOHN HUSS,
BOHEMIAN CHRISTIAN REFORMER,
MARTYRED AT THE STAKE, JULY 6, 1415,
AS RECORDED IN FOXE'S BOOK OF MARTYRS[1]

It seemed intended by the blessed providence of God that I should be blind all my life, and I thank Him for the dispensation. If perfect earthly sight were offered me tomorrow I would not accept it. I might not have sung hymns to the praise of God if I had been distracted by the beautiful and interesting things around me...Because when I get to heaven, the first face that shall ever gladden my sight will be that of my Savior.

—FANNY CROSBY,
19TH CENTURY COMPOSER OF NEARLY 9,000 HYMNS OF FAITH
INCLUDING "BLESSED ASSURANCE," "AMERICAN MISSIONARY,"
LOVER OF JESUS WHO WAS BLIND FROM INFANCY[2]

Whether we are young or old makes no difference. What are twenty or thirty or fifty years in the sight of God? And which of us knows how near he or she may already be to the goal? That life only really begins when it ends here on earth, that all that is here is only the prologue before the curtain goes up—that is for young and old alike to think about.

—Excerpt From Dietrich Bonhoeffer's
Famous Sermon About Death
"Stations On the Road to Freedom"[3]

On the morning of that day between five and six o'clock the prisoners . . . were taken from their cells, and the verdicts of the court martial read out to them. Through the half-open door in one room of the huts I saw Pastor Bonhoeffer, before taking off his prison garb, kneeling on the floor praying fervently to his God. I was most deeply moved by the way this lovable man prayed, so devout and so certain God heard his prayer. At the place of the execution, he again said a short prayer and then climbed the steps to the gallows, brave and composed. His death ensued after a few seconds. In the almost fifty years that I worked as a doctor, I have hardly ever seen a man die so entirely submissive to the will of God.

—Camp doctor
Flossenburg Concentration Camp, Germany
Where Dietrich Bonhoeffer Was Executed April 9, 1945[4]

What defines a life well lived? What defines a death well died?

It is the Beautiful Flow. It is the evidence of the Author of Life communing with His creation surging His power within flesh to do the impossible. To face death with joy. To conquer unbelievable obstacles.

What is the "flow" I am talking about? Men have longed to explain it. It is what the woman at the well was told was the living water that would never run dry (John 4). It is what Brother Lawrence called the presence of God.[5] It is what Martin Luther knew as his Mighty Fortress.[6] It is what John Wesley experienced as his heart warmer.[7] It is what Andrew Murray described as his abiding presence.[8] It is what Elisabeth Elliot called the Everlasting Arms.[9]

It is Him. Our King Jesus. Our Abba Daddy. Our Precious Holy Spirit. It is Him so alive inside us that we believe Him and know He is true. It is His awesome convicting presence that screams "No!" when we are heading toward sin and "Yes!" as He beckons us home.

It is cleansing and flowing. Bubbly and refreshing. Forceful and surging. Awesome and potent all at the same time. It is far more than I can adequately express. It is more captivating than I have ever personally known. It is eternally increasing. Not fading. Not waning.

It is fresh and dramatic. But it is also sweet, subtle, and calm.

It is Him. Reaching toward and through His children. Oh, that we could look into heaven like Stephen. Oh, to see His form right next to our Father. That is the beautiful flow. The Lover that men and women died for. The One that carried the saints of old. It is Him. Just Him...*just Him*!

Wow! This is the place in this chapter when I sincerely wish I could break into one of Fanny's worship songs. For my words are obviously not enough. Not nearly enough to convey what I believe He wants us to grasp. So let's pretend. Let's pretend I am Fanny and I wrote this song as if He sings it over our hearts even now....

> Oh children, He says. I really love you. And if you will trust Me
> I will carry you through!
> The mountains may tremble, the earth it may quake.
> But nothing, no nothing, will take My presence from you.
> You must trust Me to live through you as I said I would faith-
> fully do.
> The dark flood...it is too much for you, but it is no match for
> Me.
> I am strong.
>
> Run to Me. Run to Me, and together you will see us stand.
> I know you. I made you. I want you more than you want Me.
> What must I do to woo you again to My side?
> The dark forces I scoff at. They will not define my cherished
> Bride.
> My children, please listen.
> This is a new season. We will treasure these days in our love.

Some will turn away. I know this.

But you . . . you must not let their fear cast you aside.

You run to Me now. Just run to Me. As simply and as sincerely
as you know how.

And then watch Me put lift to your wings.

You will soar on heights you thought you could never reach.

Above the carnage. Above the confusion. Above what you just
cannot bear.

I am your river.

I am your Flood.

I am your bright morning star.

Now, My child, you must listen. For these days are not what
they seem.

My Flood.

My Presence.

My Power is released for those who will come.

This may sound radical. (But I guess if you have read this far in the book, you
know I do not shrink back from the bold and the blunt!) I believe God is stir-
ring in this nation *even right now*. To release a flood of His presence. Oh, it may
not be coming the way we thought it would come.

Every now and then, we bump into . . .

It is Him.

Our Healing Jesus.

Our Passionate Savior.

Our Truth Teller, Counselor, and Guide.

Our Lion of the Tribe of Judah.

I saw Him one day. I caught a glimpse of His Beautiful Powerful Flood, and
I knew His presence in a new way I had not known. May I take a moment and
tell you what I mean?

The Day I Saw His Beautiful Powerful Flood

I was busy doing some research. My attention was on internet stories that would fit with my writing project, when I happened upon a short video that would imprint my mind and recalibrate my soul.

It was a clip from a foreign news talk show with people who spoke a language I had trouble understanding. The host of the show was speaking with an interpreter so some of the words were English but most were in subtitles.

The mood on the show was somber yet sweetly anticipatory as the host began questioning a young man on a telephone line. It was the brother of two of the Egyptian (Coptic) Christians who had recently been beheaded by ISIS with the group of twenty-one fellow captives.

I wish I could show you the video right now. But, since I can't, I have watched it several times myself and transcribed for you what happened before my eyes. Here is the incredible dialogue in that interview. The young man on the phone was named Beshir.

> **Host:** Please tell me your feelings, Beshir.
>
> **Beshir:** I have two brothers who were killed. Martyr Bishoy Estafanos Kamel and Martyr Samuel Estafanos Kamel. I am proud of them. Bishoy is 25 years old and Samuel is 23 years old. They are a pride to Christianity. And they are my pride too. They make me walk raising my head up in pride.
>
> **Host:** (As he is shaking his head in amazement) Tell us more about your faith and your pride. We want to learn from you.
>
> **Beshir:** ISIS gave us more than we asked when they didn't edit out the part where they declare their faith and call Jesus Christ. ISIS helps to strengthen our faith.
>
> **Host:** (Still shaking his head in amazement) Wow! Great is your faith.
>
> **Beshir:** I thank ISIS because they didn't cut the audio when they screamed declaring their faith.
>
> **Host:** Great, my dear. Tell me, how is your family doing?

Beshir: Believe me when I tell you that the people here are happy and congratulating one another. They are not in a state of grief but congratulate one another for having so many from our village die as martyrs. We are proud of them.

Host: I want to know how you felt when you heard of the air strikes and when you saw the bodies of dead ISIS members.

Beshir: I will tell you frankly, since the Roman times, we as Christians have been targeted to be martyred. This only helps us to endure such crisis, because the Bible tells us to love our enemies and bless those who curse us. However, the airstrikes were a good response by the government after such a long wait after our brothers disappeared...But if they had been killed as soon as they were captured we wouldn't have cared for any retaliation....

Host: I want to ask you a question on your faith. Would you get upset or someone from your family get upset if we ask for forgiveness for those who killed your brothers?

Beshir: Forgiveness for whom?

Host: For those who slayed and killed.

Beshir: Today I was having a chat with my mother asking her what she would do if she saw one ISIS member on the street. She said this, and I'm repeating it honestly not because I'm on air! She said she would invite him home because he helped us enter the kingdom of heaven.

Host: (With sincere admiration and gentleness, he shook his head and whispered.) How beautiful.

Beshir: Believe me, these were my mother's words!

Host: I believe you, dear. I believe you!

Beshir: And she is an uneducated woman over 60 years old. I asked her, "What will you do if you see those ISIS members passing on the street, and I told you that's the man who slayed your son?" She said, "I will ask for God to open his eyes and ask him in our house because he helped us into the kingdom of God!"

Host: With this good spirit I will ask you to pray for them, the ISIS members, now that you are on air.

Beshir: (With passion in his voice) Dear God, please open their eyes to be saved and to quit their ignorance and the wrong teachings they were taught.[10]

And with that, the interview ended.

I sat there processing what I had just witnessed…my mind struggling to make sense of what I heard. In fact, I watched it three times.

At first I thought maybe it was a case of "reverse logic." That these Coptic Christians had spent so much time in the Middle East that they had a secret death wish and that is why they were talking about martyrdom as they did. But I could quickly determine that was not the explanation. There was something deeper at work, and suddenly the revelation hit my heart: These people really believed Matthew 5:10–12! I mean they thought it was literally true!

> Blessed are those who are persecuted because of righteousness, *for theirs is the kingdom of heaven.* Blessed are you when people insult you, persecute you and falsely say all kinds of evil against you because of me. Rejoice and be glad, because great is your reward in heaven, for in the same way they persecuted the prophets who were before you (emphasis added).

They really believed Matthew 5:43–45!

> You have heard that it was said, "Love your neighbor and hate your enemy." But I tell you, Love your enemies and pray for those who persecute you, that you may be children of your Father in heaven.

My heart was overcome with conviction as I began praying to my Father:

> *Lord, I don't have this kind of faith. Please forgive me! I, as a mother, cannot imagine stepping out of my own grief to have this much love for You in my heart. This is a river force of Your power that I do not often see here in the United States. There is a beauty here that is awesome. Lord, I find myself wanting what I see they have!*

What an odd thing, to be asking for what suffering ISIS-terrorized people have! But it was as if while I prayed it, I could remember what Paul said in his letter to the Philippians:

> But whatever were gains to me I now consider loss for the sake of Christ. What is more, I consider everything a loss because of the surpassing worth of knowing Christ Jesus my Lord, for whose sake I have lost all things. I consider them garbage, that I may gain Christ and be found in him, not having a righteousness of my own that comes from the law, but that which is through faith in Christ—the righteousness that comes from God on the basis of faith. I want to know Christ—yes, to know the power of his resurrection and participation in his sufferings, becoming like him in his death, and so, somehow, attaining to the resurrection from the dead.
>
> —PHILIPPIANS 3:7–11

This is a whole different brand of Christianity from what I have been raised to experience.

This is not worship music, soft lights, gentle testimonies, or feel-good experiential faith. This is raw, beautiful power infused with incredible supernatural hope. This is knowing Him in a whole new way. Not just in the happy resurrection time, but in the costly fellowship of His sufferings!

Could this be what our God is flowing to American Christians right now?

This would be the answer to all of our problems! This would be all that we are longing for and more! And yes, I do believe this is what He is pouring out to those who want to step into His flood.

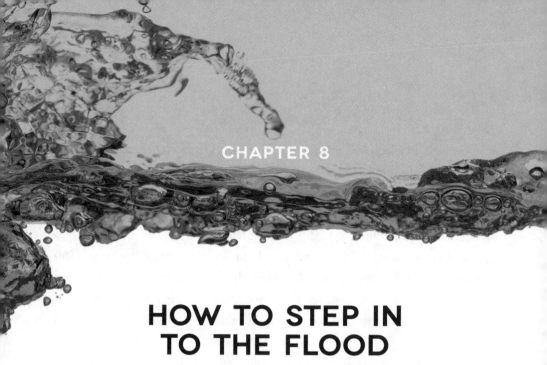

CHAPTER 8

HOW TO STEP IN TO THE FLOOD

Yes, the true church is one that is burning hot in love with her Bridegroom.

—John Burton,
The Coming Church[1]

I was tucked away in a little cabin out on the Oklahoma plain. No interruptions from the world to disturb me, I had left home on an important mission. I was going to write this book. I was there to hear my Father's voice so I could pen the words that He would inspire.

But as I sat there at my desk I had one problem. I was very nervous. I had laid my heart out before Him in eager anticipation, realizing that without His presence my labors would be for naught. Doubts were knocking on my mind. What if I pray and I feel nothing? What if I go out to seek God, and I have to call back home and report He was nowhere to be found? I am embarrassed to admit this problem, but I am guessing I might not be the only one who has these kinds of troubling thoughts. Sure, I knew those stories we read about in the last chapter about great heroes of the faith who heard God's voice and faced death without appearing to doubt. But, as I sat there in my little cabin, I was distinctly aware of a simple fact: I am not Dietrich Bonhoeffer, and I am certainly not John (or Jane) Huss. I am just…me.

How would I ever have the kind of ISIS-resistant faith we were talking about? I was having trouble facing a blank computer screen and believing my God could show up to help. That is when my Heavenly Father reminded me of something so simple I could've missed it among my noisy doubts.

"Lisa, this is not about you. This is about Me!"

And I knew just what He was talking about. I would not be able to perform my way into His Beautiful Flood. I would only be able to jump into His Flood by faith. That was so comforting to my nervous heart! Here is the truth: Our God is ready to bring us into the place of His power. If we will trust Him, and want Him, and choose Him, He will come…by faith.

In this chapter we are going to talk about stepping into this Flood the Lord is sending. But before I start to elaborate I want to nail this down very clearly. It will only come by faith.

We will not work our way into His Flood, and we will not bargain our way in either. We will only step in because we believe. That is it. If we really believed God wanted to pour over our lives a new wave of His presence that would cause us to stand under the pressures of the dark flood, why would we not step into His river by faith? I thought of three things that might keep us out:

- The counterfeits
- The cost
- The cross

Let's take a little effort to see what these three things are.

The Counterfeits

In America today we like to talk a lot about God, but sometimes it seems we want Him on our own terms. We worship Him for what He can do for us rather than for who He is. And before we know it, we have created a god in our own image that is a cheap counterfeit to the true God of the Bible.

I saw an article from *The Huffington Post* article this past week titled "Churches Could Fill Their Pews With Millennials If They Just Did This."[2] I was interested to see what the *The Huffington Post* religious editors would consider the way to fill the churches. One glance at the article, and it was easy to see. They wanted a Jesus makeover. They wanted me to turn Jesus into a social justice superhero who would connect with their political causes.

Sorry. But we are not going to be able to re-brand Jesus. I don't care who is going to come to church! God is not like Toyota who might be looking for a trendy makeover. When we play with these ideas, we are endangering our faith.

Counterfeits are all around us. We will talk more about them in section three of this book. But the counterfeits of false doctrine and egocentric, feel-good, bless-me-faith are not going to stand under fire. That is what Jesus warned of in Matthew 24 when He talked about the love of most growing cold due to the increase in wickedness. If we want the new Flood, we will need to trade in our cheap counterfeits.

The Cost

I wonder what would happen if Dietrich Bonhoeffer were alive today and tried to get a publishing company to take his book *The Cost of Discipleship.*[3] I wonder if the marketing team would only agree to take the book if he gave it a title change. Maybe something like *The Blessing of Discipleship* would make for stronger book sales.

Think about it. We twenty-first century Americans like books on grace. We like songs about blessings and love. We are not too keen on suffering, and we have not particularly been interested in the "cost of discipleship." Is it possible that we have been duped into a spineless faith simply because we failed to reckon with this word *cost*? Jesus outlined our cost pretty clearly when He said we would need to deny ourselves, lose our lives, and be hated.

The Cross

We won't be able to step in to the Beautiful Flood unless we have already been transformed by the cross. It is pretty basic really. If a person is not truly in Christ, he will not be able to partake of His Holy Spirit presence. So that leads us to an obvious question. Are the people who are calling themselves Christians today really Christians?

Many would have to wonder when we consider the many studies that we will consider in this book that show the beliefs and behaviors of those who say they are in Christ. Obviously, only God can judge the true condition of a human heart. However, this I know: Jesus Himself warned in Matthew 7:22 of many who will call Him "Lord, Lord," but He will say to them, "I never knew you; depart from me." The cross is a branding. It is not a necklace design. A true conversion is a decision for Lordship. It marks the identity of the worshiper. The old man is crucified, and the new man is born again. Holiness becomes the desire. Purity and relationship with Him becomes the passion.

Perhaps it is time to evaluate how many of those who are claiming Christ are not really in Christ at all. They are having a form of religion, but are not true disciples. Obviously, if someone is not a true Christian, the Flood will make no real sense.

God sent His Son to pay the perfect cost for our sins. He loves us and wants all of us to come to Him via the cross and its completed work.

It is possible someone who is reading this book right now is not a true follower of Christ. If so, I pray that you come to Jesus honestly and give Him your life today. I would love to help you find a confidence in your salvation. Please, if I am speaking to you, go to our website and click on our link that says "Need Jesus." (Also, please go to the end of this book for more information.)

So, let's say we have eliminated all three of the hindrances I named. We have stepped out from our counterfeits, counted the cost of discipleship and come to the cross for salvation. How then do we step in to the Powerful Flood? That brings us back to our first answer. We step in by faith. Faith is the leaning of the entire self upon the confidence of who He is and what He has promised. It is not goose bumps and feelings. It is rock solid and immovable because He and His Word are immovable.

You will be ready to step into the Flood by faith once you are convinced He is calling you toward Him. That is why I want us to read over each of the following verses.

> But if from there you seek the LORD your God, you will find him if you seek him with all your heart and with all your soul.

—DEUTERONOMY 4:29

Ask and it will be given to you; seek and you will find; knock and the door will be opened to you.

—MATTHEW 7:7

The LORD is good to those whose hope is in him, to the one who seeks him.

—LAMENTATIONS 3:25

Seek the LORD while he may be found; call on him while he is near.

—ISAIAH 55:6

The lions may grow weak and hungry, but those who seek the LORD lack no good thing.

—PSALM 34:10

Are you sensing hope arising? Keep reading!

Those who know your name will trust in you, for you, LORD, have never forsaken those who seek you.

—PSALM 9:10

Blessed are those who keep his statutes and seek him with all their heart.

—PSALM 119:2

Come near to God and he will come near to you.

—JAMES 4:8a

God did this so that they would seek him and perhaps reach out for him and find him, though he is not far from any one of us."

—ACTS 17:27

Ok…are you convinced yet?

If you seek him, he will be found by you.

—1 CHRONICLES 28:9

> Call to me and I will answer you and tell you great and unsearchable
> things that you do not know.
>
> —JEREMIAH 33:3

> I sought the LORD, and he answered me; he delivered me from all my
> fears.
>
> —PSALM 34:4

> My heart says of you, "Seek his face!" Your face, LORD, I will seek.
>
> —PSALM 27:8

Don't stop! We are building our faith as we read!

> Trust in the LORD and do good; dwell in the land and enjoy safe pasture.
> Take delight in the LORD, and he will give you the desires of your heart.
> Commit your way to the LORD; trust in him and he will do this: He
> will make your righteous reward shine like the dawn, your vindication
> like the noonday sun.
>
> —PSALM 37:3–6

> Then you will call on me and come and pray to me, and I will listen
> to you.
>
> —JEREMIAH 29:12

Is that not the most awesome news you have ever heard? God wants to flood
us with His power and presence. He is simply waiting for His bride to want
Him enough to ask! Do you believe it yet, my friend? Through every season
God yearns to draw near to His children. He sees the pressures building in our
lives. And He is yearning to respond.

He is waiting for someone to take Him at His word.

Hebrews 11:6 says it like this: "And without faith it is impossible to please
God, because anyone who comes to him must believe that he exists and that he
rewards those who earnestly seek him."

Simple trust.

Nothing is standing in the way of you receiving from your Father. So why
don't you go ahead and step in right now! Take a few minutes and respond to
the Lord's invitation. He is waiting to receive your prayers.

CHAPTER 9

THE STANDARD

Now when Daniel learned that the decree had been published, he went home to his upstairs where the windows opened toward Jerusalem. Three times a day he got down on his knees and prayed, giving thanks to His God, just as he had done before.

—Daniel 6:10

In the West we have a superhero fascination. We love to create movies of super-human beings who throw their bodies in front of runaway freight trains to prevent a little child being crushed on the railway tracks. We like big, green, super-muscular men who can pick up a bad guy's car with one hand and stop a speeding bullet with the other.

The Confident Hope

Those are the type of story lines that make for box office smashes and big smiles on moviegoers' faces. People inherently love the triumph of the good guy mixed with the crushing of the villain.

I think that is one reason Isaiah 59:19 stands out as one of those verses we are intrinsically excited to quote:

> So shall they fear the name of the LORD from the west, and his glory from the rising of the sun. When the enemy shall come in like a flood, the Spirit of the LORD shall lift up a standard against him.
>
> (KJV)

It is a verse that makes us swell with pride. Kind of a "my God is bigger than your God" feeling makes us feel comforted and also courageous. Like we are on the winning team in the game of life!

Many Bible scholars over the ages have tried to mine out of this verse the many nuances of the original Hebrew text to discover the full meaning of what God is saying here. And since this verse is central to our understanding of the second flood that is countering the dark flood on the earth today, I decided to wade deeper to see what great men and women of God had learned about it. Hang with me while we carefully dissect this verse because an important anchor for us today is contained in this passage.

The longer I studied, the more convinced I became that the core meaning of the verse is pretty much what the simple words say:

No matter what kind of dark force tries to move in and destroy God's people, God will eventually stop it, and His ways will prevail. I guess you could say that is a Bible commentary according to Lisa! So perhaps you might want to read it from someone with a more authoritative voice. John Gill's *Exposition of the Bible Commentary* records this about the part of the verse that says "When the enemy shall come in like a flood" (Isa. 59:19):

> "When the enemy shall come in like a flood; when Satan, the common 'enemy' of mankind, the avowed and implacable enemy of Christ and his people, 'shall come' into the world, and into the church, as he will in the latter day; and has already entered 'like' an impetuous flood, threatening to carry all before him, introducing a flood of immorality and profaneness, as in the days of Noah and Lot, to which the times of the Son of Man's coming are likened, Luke 17:26, or else a flood of error and heresy of all sorts; see Revelation 12:15 and likewise a flood of persecution, as will be at the slaying of the witnesses."[1]

Please notice how Gill's commentary hits all of our themes we have been working on. He compares the dark flood to the days of Noah and Lot. He also says that the later flood would be not of water but of immorality, profaneness, error, and heresy. Gill continued his commentary of this verse explaining what God meant by the phrase "the Spirit of the Lord shall lift up a standard against him."

Here is what he says: "Christ and his Gospel, or Christ the standard lifted up in the ministry of the Gospel; Isaiah 11:10, a set of ministers shall be raised up, having the everlasting Gospel, which they shall publish to all nations, and which shall have an universal spread; and by means of which the earth shall be filled with the knowledge of the Lord as the waters cover the sea; and which will be a sufficient check to the enemy's flood of immorality, error, and persecution; and which, after this, shall be no more" (see Revelation 14:6).

At first glance that explanation may seem confusing. Gill is saying that the Lord will raise up against the dark flood (i.e. the error and immorality and persecution) a counterbalancing force. That counterbalancing force is the everlasting Gospel that shall be shared throughout the earth by faithful ministers. So we see here a mighty declaration. Yes, the enemy will spread his flood, but at the same time God will raise up a force that defeats the darkness.

This is good news! He is clearly saying *Jesus wins!* The end of the story of mankind, the end of the drama of which we are all earthly participants is already predetermined. Our hope is restored! The flood of darkness—which is lawlessness—cannot shake the story line. The deception of people attempting to coexist their way into the Kingdom does not change the outcome. The standard of our God has been raised, and all the earth will know.

This should bring a smile to our faces and a comfort to our souls! It is better than a superhero tale. We need to be reminded of this. *Nothing can stop God's force.* Nothing!

This is confirmed in New Testament passages also:

> On this rock I will build my church, and the gates of Hades [i.e. hell] will not overcome it.
>
> —MATTHEW 16:18 (emphasis added)

Who shall separate us from the love of Christ? Shall trouble or hardship or persecution or famine or nakedness or danger or sword? As it is written:

> "For your sake we face death all day long;
> we are considered as sheep to be slaughtered."

No, in all these things we are more than conquerors through him who loved us. For I am convinced that neither death nor life, neither angels nor demons, neither the present nor the future, nor any powers, neither height nor depth, nor anything else in all creation, will be able to separate us from the love of God that is in Christ Jesus our Lord.

—ROMANS 8:35–39

We are talking invincible here! Unstoppable and immovable.

Of course, when we read these verses our hearts will try to argue. But God, John Huss was burned at the stake and the Jews, Your chosen people, were slaughtered by the millions at the hands of Nazis. How can You claim victory in the midst of those defeats?

We must be willing to answer that question through the eyes of the Eternal Kingdom instead of through the eyes of our temporary earthly one. That is what the heroes of the faith were able and willing to do as recorded in Hebrews 11:39: "These were commended for their faith, yet none of them received what had been promised." They did not see the final chapter in their lifetime, yet they still believed. One day Jesus will return, and all the nations will bow.

So let's put this all together.

It is as if God were declaring to our generation as He has in generations of old.

Everyone will eventually know this from one end of the earth to the other: When the enemy of God advances with his flood of darkness, the Spirit of God will always raise up the standard that comes against his darkest efforts. And God's side, the Kingdom of Heaven, will ultimately win.

If the body of Christ were to get hold of the full meaning of these passages right now, we would see an amazing surge in bold, confident living in the flow of the beautiful flood! Fear would vanish. Faith would arise. The news of the day would not shake us as we remember that not even death could stop our victory.

That is what I call an awesome standard of hope.

So what is a "standard" anyway?

If you notice, we did a whole discussion of Isaiah 59:19 previously and talked all about the "standard" that God would raise up, but we never defined exactly what a "standard" is.

In parallel verses in the Old Testament to our key text in Isaiah, sometimes the word *banner* is interchanged for the word *standard*. In that day the banner was the signage or emblem that was taken out in front of an army as they went to war. It was a sign to all that identified the army.[2]

Here is an example from the eleventh chapter of Isaiah 10–12:

> In that day the Root of Jesse will stand as a *banner* for the peoples; the nations will rally to him, and his resting place will be glorious. In that day the Lord will reach out his hand a second time to reclaim the remnant of his people from Assyria, from Lower Egypt, from Upper Egypt, from Cush, from Elam, from Babylonia, from Hamath and from the islands of the Mediterranean.
>
> He will raise a *banner* for the nations and gather the exiles of Israel; he will assemble the scattered people of Judah from the four quarters of the earth (emphasis added).

In this passage, Jesus Himself (who is the Root of Jesse) stands as a banner. That reminds us of what the New Testament declares in Philippians 2:10: "That at the name of Jesus every knee should bow, in heaven and on earth and under the earth." He is the banner, and His name is our standard against all foes.

Let's put this in a modern context. Jesus is the only real banner right now even as men attempt to make other flags to wave. The rainbow flag will not prevail. The ISIS banner will bow to the King of kings and the Lord of lords. It is settled and will not change even as the schemes of men seem to be making progress in our generation.

We Are the Standard!

We are not left to wonder how this all fits together. The Bible makes it pretty clear: there are two floods, two opposing forces, and two Kingdoms. And, praise God, there is one unshakable plan!

Father God has this. He is not waiting on us to "fix the dark flood." He already took care of the darkness. Colossians 2:15 says: He "disarmed the powers and authorities, he made a public display of them, triumphing over them by the cross." He is simply waiting on us to jump in to the river of His own flood so that together we may crush our foe.

But we are not complete with our understanding of the standard yet.

You see, in actuality if Christ is living in us and He is the standard, then by very definition we are that standard too!

Can you see it? When the enemy comes in like a dark flood, God is raising *us* up as a standard against it. Jesus's body—the church that is on the earth right now—is the standard.

That is why we are in such an exciting position! Think about John Huss. He was the standard against a dark flood of heresy that was pouring over his generation and keeping men from Christ. Martin Luther was the standard when he stood in the river of darkness and said no to a corrupt system of indulgences that made a mockery of a righteous and Holy God. Amy Carmichael was the standard when she rescued little girls from the Hindu flood of evil.

We are waiting to see who will be the standard in this generation.

A Glimpse of the Standard

As I was sitting in my little cabin writing this chapter a great illustration of the standard happened right on my social media feed. Someone shared with me a new BuzzFeed video that was trending on Facebook that day. Perhaps by the time you read this, as I describe it, you will all know which video I mean. Or perhaps this little video like so many others will pop up in the flood and then go back down under the river never really to be thought of again.

The video featured a group of young people making individual statements about what they believe. They each said, "I am a Christian but I am not [...]," or "I am [...]," and then they each inserted words and phrases that identified their views. One said, "I am Christian, but I am not homophobic." Another said, "I am Christian, but I am queer." Another said, "I'm not judgmental," and another, "I'm not close-minded."[3] You get the picture.

The video was obviously making a very strong statement. At first glance, the apparent sincerity of the young lives made it difficult emotionally to dismiss them. The flood was working quite effectively with a mysterious power to deceive. I wondered to myself who would get sucked in to their words. I didn't have to wonder for long as I noted who of my friends were liking the page. My heart was broken again, and I found myself crying out in fear for the souls of those now trapped.

But that's when someone called my attention to the other comments the video was receiving. Buried down in the massive lists of affirmations were words like these:

> "Being a Christian is about following Jesus. He was never
>   mentioned in this video. No sin. Nor salvation."
> "This video is frustrating...and wrong."
> "I will believe God, not what society says I ought to believe."
> Sum of this video is: "I'm a Christian, yet I don't follow Christ,"
>   said a young man named Timothy.
> Sierra says: "Basically...Hi, I'm a Christian, but I cherry-pick
>   the Bible."
> Karen says: "When you're a Christian, you shouldn't feel the
>   need to say, '"But I'm....' You're either Christian or you're
>   not."

One of the funniest responses was someone who said that they were not a Christian, but they were pretty sure the people in the video were not either! *Hmm.* Does that say something? So what was happening in social media that day? God was raising up a standard in the midst of the flood. No, a more accurate way to put it is this:

Each of those who dared to step into the dark flood river *became the standard*!

Can you see it? It was as if the river was rushing full stream when someone dared to wade out in it, stand firm, and let some of the flow deflect off them so the river was interrupted. Oh God, that others would step in to the river at this hour! Oh, that Your children would so trust that Your standard will hold that we would banish all fear of man and be Your standard. We would be Your light set upon a hill so that those who want to know You can find their way home!

I am proud of those who were willing to step out and say "no" to the deception on their social media posts. It was a good start. But I am thinking the pressure against us will be much more than just replying on a Facebook feed! If we are to be the standard we will need to be receiving the flood of His power like never before.

If we are to be that standard in our generation, we need unshakable confidence in the promise that the Lord makes to us. Let's take that up in our next chapter.

CHAPTER 10

THE PROMISE THAT WILL NEVER FAIL

America's grown-ups, who have the ability to influence and pray for the young Christians, must not declare defeat and give up on us.

—Chelsen Vicari,
Distortion: How the New Christian Left Is Twisting the Gospel and Damaging the Faith[1]

The young preacher evangelist found himself discouraged and at the point of giving up. On the outside he kept up a good appearance. But on the inside it felt to him like his whole ministry was a flop. Doubts were plaguing him day and night, and it did not help when one of his good friends tried to provide him some "encouragement." His friend Charles Templeton was a good man attempting the same mission as the young evangelist: to impact his generation for Jesus. But Charles had chosen a different path for his career advancement. While the young evangelist had hit the road preaching, Charles had pursued an advanced degree at Princeton University.

Believing he had discovered something his friend would want to know, Charles set up a meeting with the evangelist. Charles had concluded that the Bible was flawed. His professors taught Charles that if he and his colleagues really wanted to preach and help humanity, they would accept the new academic version of Christianity. They had "corrected" the biblical errors to bring answers to the world's toughest problems.

Maybe Charles is right, the young preacher mused. Maybe all the frustrations of not seeing the "break-through" in my ministry would be fixed if I followed Charles's path and pursued a higher education degree. It made some sense to his natural mind. Do I really believe the Bible is authoritative? There are so many questions I cannot answer.

During a preaching assignment at a retreat center named Forrest Home, his internal conflict came to a head. As he prepared for his meetings, he searched his Bible for answers. A repetitive phrase in the Scriptures caught his attention: "Thus sayeth the Lord.... Thus sayeth the Lord...." He had always before accepted those words as trustworthy. But in the flood of his confusion, he would have to redecide what to do with not only those words but also the entire Bible. Was it divinely powerful and settled as eternally true?

Struggling, he left his room to walk into the woods. As he set his Bible on a nearby tree stump, that place became his defining altar as he cried out from the depth of his heart:

> O God! There are many things in this book I do not understand. There are many problems with it for which I have no solution. There are many seeming contradictions. There are some areas in it that do not seem to correlate with modern science. I can't answer some of the philosophical questions Chuck and others are raising.

And then as he found himself falling to his knees, the Beautiful Flood waters enveloped him, and he found himself praying again:

> Father, I am going to accept this as Thy Word—by faith! I'm going to follow faith to go beyond my intellectual questions and doubts, and I will believe this to be Your inspired Word!

And, as they say, the rest is history. That man was the renowned evangelist Billy Graham whose ministry has led millions to the Lord.

As he recorded in his autobiography, *Just As I Am*, Billy Graham experienced the power and presence of God with him that day as he stood up from his stump altar and tears fell from his eyes. He knew he had been changed by the power of the One he would faithfully serve.[2]

The transformation in his ministry was immediate. The next day as he spoke at Forrest Home four hundred people made a decision for Christ, and the friend who had invited him to that event reported that he preached with a new authority she had never seen before.

We Are in the Same Boat

We find ourselves in the same position as our brother Billy Graham. We will have to decide what to do with the Bible. Every day—in fact even this very day as I am penning this chapter—we read of our friends who are changing their beliefs. Why? Because they are adjusting and altering in an attempt to make sense of the dark flood that is sweeping over them and trying to drag them and their loved ones away. And as we listen to their words, just as Billy Graham did, we find ourselves tempted toward their reasonings, such as:

- God is love, so He would never condemn a person to hell.
- No one says we have to believe in a literal ark and flood to know Jesus and make it to heaven.
- Satan and his demons were mythological explanations of ancient people that did not know germ theory.
- The Bible is really important. Really. But not all parts are correct for today's modern world.
- My grandmother believed it completely only because she did not have the education I have.
- Jesus never mentioned the word *homosexual*.
- Real love would never call homosexuality a sin.
- Judging is against the Bible so how can anyone say what is right or wrong for someone else?

What is happening to us is just what Billy Graham faced out on his stump. We are wrestling with whether the Bible is a "Thus sayeth the Lord" or simply a nice, optional suggestion. And what we decide could—and very well might—shake nations.

What Do We Do With Our Doubts?

I thought for this section I would get a personal testimony from my twenty-four-year-old son, Lucas, as just this past summer he wrestled with this issue.

Lucas's story:

Recently, I was asked to speak at my church for the Sunday morning service. When I heard the topic my first response was, "Oh, this should be fairly easy to prepare for." You see, I have had the pleasure of speaking at many churches, conferences, youth events, etc., over the past few years, and I thought this would be similar to the many times I had spoken before. The topic I was assigned to speak on was, "The Validity and Reliability of Scripture."

For my academic mind (and having just completed my master's degree), I figured I would pull some outline out of a great apologist's work in a couple hours and "voila!" my message would be ready. I mean, how hard could it be?

Fourteen hours and sixty-six PowerPoint slides later, my preparation was complete, and I was ready to deliver my "Seven Reasons We Can Trust the Bible" teaching.

That weekend of studying did something inside of me that I will forever be grateful for. You see, as I have moved into my mid '20s I have watched friend after friend turn their back on the Word of God and fall into the progressive Christianity mind set of my generation. I did not expect my non-Christian friends to follow the Word of God, but these were my Christian friends who were throwing out their Bibles! The ones with whom I had gone on missions trips to Brazil, Dominican Republic, etc.! The ones to whom I taught Sunday School and were raised in Christian homes.

I know what my Christian friends have encountered. I feel the pull every day to slowly change my beliefs in the Word of God.

Creation? That's outdated.

Traditional marriage? That's a cultural construct.

History? We know more about man's roots than the Bible shows.

I have sat in the secular college classes where professors deliberately under-mined Biblical faith. I know what it is like to have questions. Somehow as a generation we have lost the ability to anchor our faith. We are vulnerable to new whims of science and new ideas of man. I can feel the temptations knocking against my own mind to conform. It is a spiritual warfare tactic to try and intimidate us to let hold of truth.

But we do not have to bow to the pressures. We can learn the truth. I may not be a professional apologist with a PhD in hermeneutics, but here are seven things I settled on.

Seven Reasons We Can Trust the Bible

1. Historical Evidence
2. Scientific Accuracy
3. Predictive Accuracy
4. Author Consistency
5. Cultural Consistency
6. Motive Authenticity
7. Test of Time

I would love to share with you all the information that I found, but that would take up too much space in this book! I would be happy to share with you my PowerPoint and a podcast if you are like me and need to boost your faith. Go to frontlinefamilies.org for the resource.

Back to Lisa for a Final Challenge

If we have questions, rest assured, God has answers! I am so grateful for Lucas's testimony. Doubts can be a doorway to greater faith if we press in to the Lord and build confidence in His Word. This chapter is sitting right here in the middle of the second section of this book for a reason. It is critically important to settle this question *before* we go any further!

This is your action step: Take an honest assessment of your own life. You have learned about the reality of the dark flood. You have caught the wave of the Lord's powerful flood and maybe even determined you will wade into the flood and be the standard in your generation. But have you passed the Billy Graham moment test? Have you settled your faith in the Bible? Are you ready to be sifted and tried?

If not, take Lucas up on the challenge. Pray. Study. Settle the questions. And you will drop your anchor into the only Word that I am 100 percent convinced will hold?

CHAPTER 11

THE ARK WE ARE
PERMITTED TO BUILD

By faith Noah…

—Hebrews 11:7

The date was December 31, 1999. Here is how *Time* magazine tells their story:

> As police throughout the world secured emergency bunkers for themselves, the *TIME* magazine and Time Inc. information-technology staff set up a generator-powered "war room" in the basement of the Time & Life Building, filled with computers and equipment ready to produce the magazine in case of a catastrophic breakdown of electricity and communications," explained then-assistant managing editor Howard Chua-Eoan, in a note that appeared in the magazine's commemorative 1/1/00 issue.[1]

What were these crazy people doing? They were preparing for the disaster of Y2K (or I should say the non-disaster).

Maybe you were a part of the millennium frenzy when many were predicting massive international disaster when computers worldwide would not know how to handle the date change from the last day of 1999 to the first day of 2000. There were people from all walks of life who were concerned, some to the point of storing food rations and building disaster shelters.

In the Christian world, I remember how many were listening to the world experts on the evening news but also listening to would-be spiritual prophets who proposed the Y2K event could have spiritual end-times significance as well. Some tried to tie the world crisis to Jesus coming back or the rise of anti-Christ forces.

Even if you are too young to remember this event and are not up on your history, you could probably surmise that nothing happened with the Y2K threat. We sat around our televisions watching the ball come down in Times Square on that New Year's Eve night waiting for cataclysmic reports that never materialized. We were simply left with Y2K jokes and a garage full of emergency supplies.

I think the whole event had greater impact than its $100 billion price tag. The Y2K phenomenon launched a new era of cynicism in our Christian world. Many of us began to distance ourselves from what looked like end times paranoia.

However, Scripture is full of examples of why cynicism is not proper for God's people. In fact, it will get us into trouble. Matthew warns us to keep watch because we do not know when the Lord will appear (Mt. 25:13; 24:42). First Thessalonians 5 says to be awake and alert. Second Peter 3 warns us to be on our guard. And those are just a few of the many examples. I find no place in the Bible that encourages us to grow cynical and act as if everything is okay. Jesus is coming back, and we are seeing more and more prophetic signs being fulfilled. So, if anything, we have more reason to live alert lives not less reason. (Even if we did miss it on Y2K, the Blood Moons did not pan out either.)

This is a place of revelation for the mature believer: Until we go to heaven or Jesus comes back, we are commanded to live life on the alert, believing that at any moment the Lord may appear. But we are also to live life preparing the church as if He will not be back for many generations. This is the place of balanced Biblical faith. So how do we do that in the midst of a major flood of evil?

Building Modern Arks

We need a new strategy. Or maybe what we need is a new vision. Let me paint a picture for you of what I mean. I believe God is calling us to build modern-day arks. Obviously, I am not talking about literal boat construction. I am painting a word picture for you of an adjustment in viewpoint, a strategy of living that will help us step in to this new season in confidence and strength.

As I was writing about the dark flood, I was tempted to think of ways to escape. Maybe you have done the same, where you dream of where you would run to if America fell apart or times got really dangerous. There are actually super-rich people who are making plans in case of civil unrest or economic collapse. A financial professional who works with the ultra-rich is quoted as saying, "I know hedge-fund managers who are buying airstrips in places like New Zealand because they think they need a getaway."[2]

When I talk about building arks, that is not the image I am going for. We are not building a bunker mentality to hole up in. We are building a floating place of refuge where we can survive the dark flood and yet still fulfill the great commission to lead others to Christ.

Below is a picture with a key scripture to catch where we are going with this:

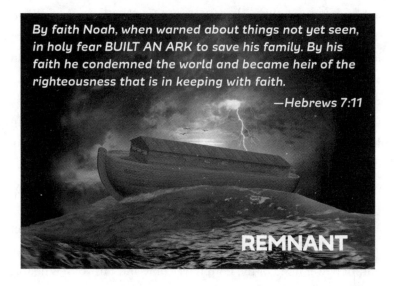

By faith Noah, when warned about things not yet seen, in holy fear BUILT AN ARK to save his family. By his faith he condemned the world and became heir of the righteousness that is in keeping with faith.

—Hebrews 7:11

REMNANT

Look at the verse from Hebrews. Noah had been warned about a flood. God had given him a blueprint and a set of instructions. He feared the Lord, so he exactly followed those directions. And because he was obedient, his whole family was saved. It is interesting how this verse uses the word *family*. It does not say that mankind was saved. It says *family*.

Family is a loaded word in our world today! In fact, ever since we named our ministry Frontline Family Ministries we have learned how difficult family ministry is. For while we all like to think warm fuzzies about the word *family*, many of us are struggling in our homes and relationships so much that we are overwhelmed when someone wants to talk to us about family. But here is the reality: God organized humans at the most basic level via family groups. Husband and wife with descendants were the pattern. And so when God looked to save a group to repopulate after judgment, He started again with the first remnant family.

Here is my bold statement: God still wants to use families. Still. Yes, we are a broken mess, but God is not going to start a new system. We will live life somewhere, and we will do most of our living out of our homes with whatever family we have around.

(Yes, I do know that many of us are single. But that does not change the fact that God wants us to hold on to the value of family relationships. That is why the devil is fighting the family image so hard! If you are single, think about your extended family and also think about your household where you live and "do" life with others.)

God wants us to build arks. He wants us to have places of refuge from the storms of the flood. We need places where we can come home after a long day of defending our faith and guarding our hearts to get some refreshing, some spiritual support, and some help. Each Christian is called to be a standard. That is hard work. In fact, it is overwhelming if you do not have the support in your life to stay strong and stay encouraged.

An ark is a place of unity where tough faith questions can be asked and hard problems can be solved. It is also a place of laughter and hope. It is a place where the beautiful power flood of the Lord is welcome and His voice is honored. It is a place of worship and a place of healing.

It sounds awesome doesn't it? Kind of like an oasis in the midst of a desert.

I want you to know that I was worried to write this section. I was concerned some of you would close this book and throw it on the floor. Your family may be so far away from an oasis it makes you want to cry (or scream). Here is my humble plea: please keep reading. God still has a plan of help for you!

We need arks. We yearn for arks. We want arks where we can live with our mission team members who share our passion to live life for the King. We desire to have lives that count in this critical hour. Think of it like this: Just imagine if church parking lots on Sunday mornings were filled with arks instead of cars. What if people came to church ready to share their strength with others rather than coming splintered and broken.

Can you imagine it? Good. Because catching a vision for it is the first place to start. Some of us, with help, can step into the vision the way I just cast it. Some of us cannot. So look at it like this. If you are single or you are the only strong believer in your home, God still wants you to have an ark. Perhaps your ark is a small group of people from your church. Perhaps it is your extended family you skype with in the evenings. But somehow He is placing us all in arks.

Do you remember the quote we read at the beginning of chapter four that talked about how Christians are living as exiles in their own country? The writer of that article, Rod Dreher, as he was exhorting Christians to find a new way to preserve the Christian faith in their families, talked about the "Benedict option."[3]

Benedict of Nursia was a pious young Christian during the time of the fall of the Roman Empire. He left his culture and went to the woods to pray. Dreher writes, "Throughout the early Middle Ages, Benedict's communities formed monasteries, and kept the light of faith burning through the surrounding cultural darkness. Eventually, the Benedict monks helped refound civilization. I believe that orthodox Christians today are called to be those new and very different St. Benedicts. How do we take the Benedict Option, and build resilient communities within our condition of internal exile and under increasingly hostile conditions? I don't know. But we had better figure this out together, and soon, while there is time."[4]

Dreher has been attacked for his idea as if he is proposing we all withdraw from culture and run to a monastery. But as I have listened to him further, I think what he is talking about is valid and falls right in line with the concept I see called "building arks." And I agree, now is the time to figure this out![5]

As we move toward the third section of our book this is the image we will pull forward with us. We are ark builders. We are looking to make the practical adjustments to position ourselves to stay in the flood of God's presence while we live as His standard and rescue those who need to know their God.

Go back and look at that picture of the ark once again. Notice the first two words of the scripture from Hebrews 11:7.

By faith Noah…

There it is again like we have seen it over and over.

How will we build our arks? By faith.

Noah did not know how to build an ark, but God provided him the blueprint. We, like Noah, will each build our arks under the instruction of our Holy God. No two arks will look exactly alike, and that is okay. Each will provide the safety and support for a generation to weather a powerful flood.

We have more things to understand as we build. We will need tools and specific preparations. We will need to dump some more weights and grab some more of His grace. That is why we have the third section of this book that follows the next chapter.

CHAPTER 12

WHAT DO WE DO NOW?

My plan for this book was to help worn-out weary Christians find a place of hope in the midst of a raging flood. I wanted to alert people and warn them, and then lead them by the power of the Holy Spirit to the One who wants to restore beauty for their ashes and hope for their traumatized hearts. I worked on those goals in sections one and two.

But after that I planned to answer the questions that I feel are in many people's minds: In light of the dark flood...What do we do now? What specific things do we change? What practical preparations do we make? And how do we build an ark?

Those are the questions people ask me every week, so I figure they needed to be addressed. I started putting together a list of ideas...and that is where I ran into my problem.

Part three of this book is called "The Preparation Plan." In this section you will find a list of twenty-four preparations (with each preparation explained in its own short chapter) in answer to our question: What do we do now? Lists can be helpful, but lists can also be dangerous. How do I know? I am the queen of lists. If you gave me a checklist of twenty-four things, I would glance at that list of preparations and make a few immediate determinations, such as: "Oh, yeah, I got that revelation in 1986. I don't need that chapter." This is pride. Or: "That chapter is way beyond me. Lisa just doesn't know what is going on in my life. My family and I are a mess." This is failure.

Can you see my dilemma? I want you to have the benefit of a great preparation checklist, but I don't want you to experience these negative traps. So here is how I solved my problem: I just exposed it.

There. That is it.

Now I feel free to go ahead and release my list since I warned you in advance of these dangers. (I recognize that in reality I might be too late. You may have already looked at the Table of Contents and fallen into one of the two traps. But that is okay. You can repent and try again! ☺ Believe me. You need this list. I need this list. We need this list much more than we probably know. So let's get started by setting the stage for part three of this book.

This next section of the book is set up to do the following things:

- Excite you
- Convict you
- Inspire you
- Equip you

Some of us love to read a book by barreling through it from cover to cover. That is me. I tackle my books and dissect them as if they were a project to kill. (*Hmm.* Do you think that might be my personality spilling out? ☺) I have stacks and stacks of books that I "read." But you will rarely catch me reading them cover to cover. I hit, attack, and am gone on to the next prey.

If that is how you want to tackle the rest of this book, go right ahead.

But some people are more like my husband, Doug. He can get one favorite book and potentially savor it for many years. His all-time favorite is *Abide in Christ* by Andrew Murray.[1] He carries it with him, highlights it, dog-ears it, and memorizes certain sections. And God has brought him amazing layers of revelation year after year. (Now, I don't want to get myself in trouble here and say that is the only book Doug has read, but I think you get my point!)

Some of us like microwave reading... and others like slow-cooker reading.

So I give you permission to do with this book whatever fits your style—with this word of caution. Microwave or speed reading is fine, but there is no such thing as a guaranteed speedy revelation. Sometimes the Holy Spirit has His own pace.

Do not gloss over when the Lord says to tarry. You might find that the exact preparation you thought you already had is the one that He wants to update and improve!

You will notice that some of these preparations are follow-ups to our Dark Flood section and some of them are follow-ups to the Beautiful Flood section. Preparation seven, about persecution, is particularly vital and will be best received after the first six preparations. I do not claim this to be an exhaustive list of all preparations needed in this hour. But it is a good starting point. For to live in relationship with our Father is to live a life of continual preparation and growth.

Do not be frustrated or discouraged if one of these chapters is not right for you now. Simply set it aside and read on. You will know when and if God wants to bring that chapter back to you at another time.

Each of the preparation chapters will end with a list of action steps. Please prayerfully consider how to apply these to your personal life. Perhaps you are reading this book in a small group setting or perhaps you are sharing this resource in a family ark building devotional time. The actions steps become your growing points. As you dive into them, I pray you will find the growth you are longing for.

Obviously, as I write this I am not able to know what new things have happened in our world since we put this resource to print. What I am showing you is not dependent on exact circumstances and ebbs and flows of this dark flood. These are timeless truths that will grow us up and make us ready to stand.

However, having said that, I recognize that world events are shifting very quickly. Know that even as this book goes to print, I will be writing to update our plans. You will find on our website at frontlinefamilies.org links that correspond to these various preparation points. I will do my best to link you to helpful resources we are using in our lives to learn to stand strong.

I must make a disclaimer on all our links and referrals. I do not personally know all the experts we link to. I cannot vouch for all of their personal doctrines or habits of holiness. I will do my best to vet our sources. But if we find out later someone has stepped in to the dark flood, we will recognize this is a risk we take in order to be in community in the body of Christ.

We truly do need each other right now as never before. Please know it is our desire to support you and your family in any practical way possible. If you have prayer needs, please contact us. If you see great resources that might help someone else, send them our way.

Together, we can build arks and stand strong until Jesus comes.

Let's get started with my personal favorite…Preparation #1!

PART THREE

THE PREPARATION PLAN

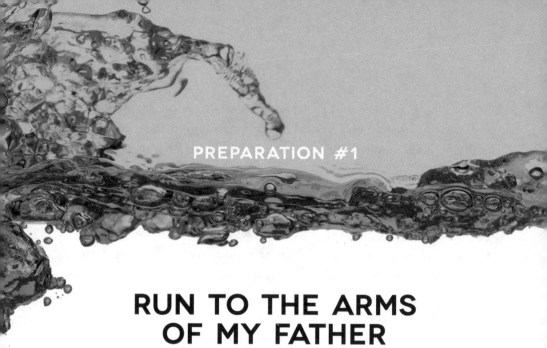

RUN TO THE ARMS
OF MY FATHER

In 1992 I found myself at an interesting place in my life. I was experiencing a personal revival with the Lord, and I was eager to serve Him and immerse myself in His ways. But I had one big challenge. I kept failing. It seemed that the harder I tried to live for Him, the more I found myself in a near-miss situation. Since I always did hate failure, I found myself wanting to hide from the only One who I really wanted to please.

It was in this season that God broke through to my heart with the simplest of revelations: What I needed was a father.

Oh, not my earthly father. I already had a wonderful one of those. What I needed was an up-close, personal relationship with my Heavenly Father. It was from Him I could receive the assurance that no one in the world could ever give. I needed to know that I was all right—failures and all. I needed to know that the big scary world around me was under His control, and by putting my trust in Him, everything would be okay. Do you know what I am talking about?

It seemed so simple to explain on paper that even a Sunday School child should have known it. I knew deep down I should already have had that peace…but I didn't. And it frustrated me. In fact, it frustrated me so much that I would try to work at believing just a little harder. And, as you might have predicted, the elusive peace seemed to get further and further from my grasp until God broke through my walls. What I was waiting for all along was not something else to do. I was waiting for something else to receive. And it was something He wanted to give me all along.

God spoke to me through a very personal form of worship music by a man named Dennis Jernigan. Dennis has a special gift of writing songs that penetrate broken hearts. Perhaps that is because his ministry and his heart of worship were birthed on the wings of his own desperation and pain. You see, Dennis as a young man had a terrible secret. He was struggling with the sin of homosexuality. But when he truly found the love of his Heavenly Father, he found freedom from his sexual sin and grew to embrace a new identity in Christ.

When I first heard Dennis sing, I felt the Father tug at my heart. Dennis disappeared and my Heavenly Father became more real to me than ever before. As I sat still in His presence, the love of the Father washed over me as my healing came. I became the little girl, and He became my Loving Daddy. All my imperfections and worries faded away.

Please do not confuse this with syrupy emotionalism; I can testify something real changed in my life that has endured to this day. That is why this revelation becomes our first preparation point: Run to the arms of your Father!

We will not make it without a radically rooted confidence in Him, our Heavenly Father. In a dark and frightening world, we need Him to fold us into His love. We must know how to run to our Father and talk to Him about our deepest needs.

One day Jesus's disciples asked Him how they should talk to God. The disciples must have noticed that Jesus knew God in a way they did not know Him. They had watched Him get up early to spend time in personal prayer, so I can imagine it was out of sincere curiosity that they said, "Hey Jesus! Would you teach us to pray?"

In answer, He could have said for them to start with: O Magnificent Great Amazing Yahweh...But instead this is how He taught them to approach their prayers: Our Father...

Let those words sink into your heart afresh. Jesus told them to come first to their Daddy.

A Gift of a Song

Dennis Jernigan is still worshiping and singing songs to draw hearts to the Father. I asked him if it would be all right if I shared one of his songs with you here in this book, just to give you a taste of what I mean. (Of course, it will be much more effective if you listen to him sing it. Go to frontlinefamilies.org to find the link.)

I Will Run to the Arms of My Father

Sometimes I make life too complicated
Sometimes I just need to stop a while
That's when I must remember
Why I was created
I must come to Father like a child

I will run to the arms of my Father
Like a lost child gladly found
Run with joy to the arms of my Father
as He lifts me from the ground
And He throws me high and He catches me
Like He can't get enough
And He laughs with me
And the look in His eye
He just loves me!

I will run to the arms of my Father
to that place where He calls me to dream
like a child who believes that his father is the best
and He's strong enough to do anything
and He makes me feel like I'm the only one
and He looks right thru me
and He says well done
and the look in His eye
He just loves me...

You love me with a love that will not let me go

thru storm or fiery trial. You love me, I know.

You love me with a love that will not let me go

Your love's like a might river

I want to get lost in the flow

I want to get lost in the flow.[1]

Are you ready to run to Father's arms? As we consider this first preparation, here are the action steps for you to consider:

Read the following Scripture verses: Matthew 18:3; Romans 8:15; Matthew 6:26, 7:11, 18:14; Luke 12:32; John 8:19; Luke 15:17; Hebrews 4:16. Let the beauty of these words flood over your soul. Meditate on them and ask the Lord to give you a revelation of Him. Here is one to get you started: "See what great love the Father has lavished on us, that we should be called children of God! And that is what we are!" (1 John 3:1).

If there was a time in your life when you had a revelation of your Father's love: Go back in your mind to the time when you knew your Father best. Perhaps you feel like you had that close relationship, but somehow under the pressures of this world it seems a distant memory. He is still right here. Today you can step back into that flow again. Retrace your steps, and remember what the Lord has done for you. You might want to dig out an old song or a an old note that you wrote to yourself. Go back to those memorial moments in your mind. It is a good thing to do. In fact, over and over in the Old Testament God called the children of Israel to set up a special memorial to remember Him.

If you have no revelations to fall back on, ask the Lord to bring you into a new revelation of Him as Daddy. He can do that for you as He did for me! Sometimes the failings of our earthly daddies get in the way of us receiving from our Heavenly Father's love. Please know God yearns to break past the limitations of your past experiences and do a big new thing in your heart. Trust Him. Ask Him. Wait for Him. He longs to draw you into His protective love.

Go to frontlinefamilies.org to find the links to Dennis Jernigan's song and other great tools to help you draw near to our Father's heart.

CHECK FOR THE ELIJAH ERRORS

Many of us want to believe we are spiritually mature. We want to believe we are "mature enough" to avoid deceptions that would wreck our lives or throw us into a ditch of pain. But are we really that "fool-proof?"[1] I am humbled to consider how many Bible characters and great men and women of history surely thought the same thing.

Errors in this life are inevitable due to our own sin nature, and the reality that we see only as through a glass rather dimly (1 Cor. 13:12). Even though mistakes and errors happen, we have the opportunity to learn from them and avoid them in the future.

Doug and I like it when our children learn from their own errors. But we like it even more when they can learn from our errors or the errors of other Godly people around them. Surely that is why God included so many not-so-pleasant details in the Bible. We have the opportunity to ask ourselves: "Where did they go wrong?"

In this chapter and the next four, we will look at the life of Elijah. Before we get into the errors Elijah made, we will need to place him in Scripture. Our story is found in 1 Kings 18 and 19.

Elijah's Story

Elijah was a mighty prophet of God for the Northern Kingdom of Israel during the reign of Ahab in the ninth century BC. By the time we pick up the story-line in 1 Kings 18, Elijah had already experienced many incredible miracles, including supernatural provisions of food and resurrections from the dead.

It was the third year of a terrible drought when the word of the Lord came to Elijah instructing him to go talk to the evil King Ahab so that the rain would come on the land. That was a scary thing for Elijah to do, because Ahab's wicked wife, Jezebel, was actively seizing and killing all the prophets in the land.

As is often the case in times of great evil, God had a secret agent working on His behalf. The secret was named Obadiah. As the servant in charge of King Ahab's palace, Obadiah was also a devout believer in the Lord. While Jezebel was busy killing off the prophets, Obadiah was busy protecting them. He took one hundred of the Lord's prophets and hid them in two different caves with enough provisions to keep them alive.

Elijah was an obedient man. Even though he found himself under threat of death, Elijah followed the Lord's command and presented himself to King Ahab. It was quite an interesting meeting between the two. When Ahab saw Elijah, he cried out to him: "Is that you (Elijah), you troubler of Israel?" (How is that for a pleasant greeting from your king? But Elijah did not shy back from the confrontation.)

> "I have not made trouble for Israel," Elijah replied, "but you and your father's family have. You have abandoned the Lord's commands and have followed the Baals. Now summon the people from all over Israel to meet me on Mount Carmel. And bring the four hundred and fifty prophets of Baal and the four hundred prophets of Asherah, who eat at Jezebel's table."
>
> —1 Kings 18:18–19

This was most certainly a courageous response. Ahab sent word throughout all Israel and assembled the prophets of Mount Carmel. Elijah went before the people and said:

"How long will you waver between two opinions? If the LORD is God, follow him; but if Baal is God, follow him." But the people said nothing.

—1 KINGS 18:21

How America Can Be Seen in This Story

As we consider this famous scene from Elijah's life, it strikes me how this famous discourse is incredibly parallel to where we find ourselves in America today. We can locate ourselves in this scene for at least four significant reasons:

1. In America, the truth gets you in trouble.

In America's politically correct environment, whoever steps up and tells the truth according to God's Word is considered a "troubler" or "hater" just as Elijah was.

2. We are a nation of Baal worshippers.

On April 23, 2001, just five months before the September 11 disaster, David Wilkerson, a well-known pastor from Times Square Church in New York City delivered a sermon titled "Seven Thousand Did Not Bow." While speaking on this passage of Scripture in 1 Kings, Wilkerson drew amazing parallels between ancient Israel and modern America:

> Baal worship, under Nimrod, originated at the Tower of Babel. This godless man declared, "Let us make us a name" (Gen. 11:4). So Babel was built as a monument to human success and accomplishment. At the top was an observatory, where astrologers followed the heavenly bodies. These proud people literally "reached for the stars."
>
> In Elijah's day, the god Baal supposedly granted its worshippers success, fame, and prosperity. Those who kissed the idol's feet sought fulfillment in every area of materialism and sensuality. Who were these Baal worshippers? They were God's chosen people, backslidden worshippers of Jehovah. Like me, you may wonder how God's people could be drawn to such blatant idolatry.
>
> Right now, the same spirit of Baal is raging in our nation. On Wall Street, in front of the U.S. Stock Exchange, we see the very image of

this pagan god. It's a bronze statue of a huge bull, representing a "bull market," ever-increasing prosperity, great wealth and fame, human achievement. These are the gods our nation bows to.[2]

Wow! That is so incredibly true!

3. We, like Israel, are wavering between two opinions.

Israel had known of their God. She had a history that revealed a God who had parted rivers and delivered their nation out of bondage. But Elijah's generation had totally forgotten who they were. Like Israel, America is in a similar wavering opinion.

4. The church in America has tried to stay silent.

The people of Israel were silent when Elijah asked them to choose between God and Baal. That was because of their entanglement with the Baal worship *and* their fear of the King! Silence seemed to them the safest option. So too in America, much of the church has attempted to go silent—some out of fear of persecution, and some out of fear of loss of fame and reputation.

We can definitely locate ourselves in this story, can we not? We can use Elijah's words to take a peek into our own lives right now.

Action Steps

Here are action steps to let the Lord speak to our hearts:

1. Get out your Bible and read 1 Kings 18 for yourself. There is power in reading directly from God's Word.

2. Evaluate the quote from David Wilkerson. How has the Baal spirit of success, prosperity, wealth, fame, and human achievement pulled on your life and the lives of your family and friends? How will you resist that seductive pull that is opposed to Jesus's call in Mark 8:34 and Matthew 23:12?

3.   Consider again the divided state of Israel. Are you, like them, wavering between two priorities in your life? If so, what will you do?

4.   Have you grown quiet in the face of increasing opposition? Would others say you have compromised your faith because of that pressure? What about the people you hang with? Have they become fearful, distracted, or silent? Quick, now is the time to repent of that sin before the Lord. Then begin praying for other believers.

COME OUT OF THE CAVE

Misperceptions. Sometimes they can get us into trouble. As we continue our discussion of Elijah, we are going to identify some of his misperceptions.

Elijah should be remembered first and foremost for his godly stand for righteousness even as others in his generation turned away. However, unfortunately for him, his own miscalculations put him under tremendous pressure. Remember in the last chapter, we found that Obadiah, unbeknownst to Ahab and Jezebel, had hidden one hundred of the Lord's prophets in caves to protect them from the king's death squads.

That is what makes the statement by Elijah in 1 Kings 18:22 rather mysterious. Here is how Scripture records it:

> Then Elijah said to them, "I am the only one of the Lord's prophets left, but Baal has four hundred and fifty prophets."

What was Elijah saying there? I guess when we all get to heaven we can ask him. Just half a chapter earlier in 1 Kings 18:13 we see that Obadiah himself told Elijah about his activities when he said:

Haven't you heard, my lord [meaning Elijah], what I did while Jezebel was killing the prophets of the LORD? I hid a hundred of the LORD's prophets in two caves, fifty in each, and supplied them with food and water.

Hmmm. Somehow Elijah's perception was not in agreement with what Obadiah said. I can think of at least three possible explanations of this unusual discrepancy:

1. Elijah did not consider these prophets to be "real prophets."

2. Elijah did not have a chance to verify the news that Obadiah had recently shared with him, so he did not believe it as fact.

3. Elijah had become so conditioned to being "alone" that he did not really receive the news about the other prophets.

Perhaps you can think of some other possibilities to add to that list. But for whatever reason, Elijah perceived he was alone and did not acknowledge God's other prophets who were hidden in the caves. In actuality, we know very little from Scripture about those men who had been hidden in those two caves. But for just a few minutes, let's focus on what we do know about them:

- They knew the Lord and had a calling on their lives to serve Him.
- They lived among a group of God's people who had been ensnared by a false worship system.
- Their messages had been silenced.
- They had been placed by God in crowded, uncomfortable caves to protect their lives.
- The caves proved to be their fortresses and places of divine provision.
- They eventually came out of their caves to help restore the land.

David Wilkerson, in that well-known sermon we looked at in the last chapter, had this to say about those men:

Think about the one hundred prophets hidden by Obadiah. They lived an isolated existence in caves for at least three to four years, during a severe famine. These men had no outside ministry. They were completely out of the public's view, forgotten by most people. They couldn't even share in Elijah's victory on Mount Carmel. No doubt, the world would call them failures, insignificant men who hadn't accomplished anything.

Yet God had given these devoted servants the precious gift of time. They had days, weeks, even years to pray, study, grow, and minister to the Lord. You see, God was preparing them for the day when He would release them to minister to His people. Indeed, these same men would shepherd those who returned to God under Elijah's ministry.[1]

Caves mentioned in the Bible were often doorways to Kingdom greatness. Think of David as he hid from Saul in 1 Samuel 22. Caves are not fun places by human standards but necessary places by God's standard. They are places where flesh dies and depth of resolve is born.

Could it be that some of us have been hidden in caves for just such an hour as this? Could it be that some of us have been in our caves for so long that we have almost forgotten why we are there? We have not had large public ministries. We are not famous. But we are among those who have faithfully been studying God's Word, praying for revival, fighting spiritual battles, and learning to hear His voice. If so, I believe the Lord is saying, "Come out of your cave! This is the hour you have been preparing for! There are people who need what you have. They need the truth. They need to be discipled. They need to know of the deeper things of God. Please come out of your cave and lead!"

To others who are just now entering your cave years, be encouraged. God knows what He is doing. If He is hiding you away right now, and if you will faithfully follow His leadership, your time of preparation will bear abundant fruit in the Kingdom. Do not grow weary and do not give up!

God has been preparing leaders for this important hour of history. It could be the true leaders who arise now in this generation will not be the famous ones who have found themselves in the limelight before. God is sorting out who will stand firm for Him and who will bow to the pressure of the dark flood. Some leaders have compromised, grown quiet, or wavered in the face of spiritual pressure. They may attract around them new crowds of people who like what they have to preach. Scripture calls this the "itching ears" phenomenon (2 Tim. 4:3).

Cave prophets, when they arrive on the scene to declare the word of the Lord, may not tickle our ears with what we want to hear. They will be clear and bold and not entangled with the narratives of the world, because they have been separated from His Word. Perhaps we had better prepare our hearts to receive them.

Surely Elijah was pleased when these men in hiding arrived on the scene to strengthen a struggling nation. And surely we will be glad when those who are called come out of their caves to lead!

Action Steps

1. Perhaps you feel like you have been in a cave hiding for many years. Perhaps you have grown cynical and grouchy in your cave and you need to repent to the Lord for your complaining discontentment. Perhaps you have even given up. If that is you, now is your time to talk to God.

2. Look around you right now. Who do you see speaking with a bold clear voice for the Lord? Stop and pray for them. Many of them, like Elijah and those one hundred prophets, are under death threats at this very hour. Recognize that, just like Elijah, these are mere human beings. They will make errors just as he did. Be ready to forgive their immaturities and pray for them to lead skillfully in God's will and timing.

3. If you are still in a cave preparing, please finish the preparation work. Only come out under the Lord's leadership. He is in charge of seasons. We need your leadership voice and your zeal, but we need you packed full of the Word of God, not packed full of man's reasonings. Pray and seek Him while He may be found. Stay faithful to what He has asked you to do.

4. If God has called you to come out of your cave and lead, now is the time to cry out for His wisdom and direction...and step out!

CONQUER FEAR

Please do not think I am being critical of our brother Elijah. He was undoubtedly one of the greatest heroes of the faith. Yet, even as he did the most amazing exploits in the Kingdom, he was still just a man subject to human frailties.

His story in 1 Kings 18 is surely one of the most exciting events of biblical history. Hollywood could not even do it justice. Eight hundred and fifty false prophets faced off to the one true prophet, Elijah. The two opposing sides gathered a pile of wood and prepared a sacrifice. Then Elijah challenged the crowd and the prophets, saying in verse 24:

> Then you call on the name of your god, and I will call on the name of the LORD. And the god who answers by fire—he is God.

The rest of the story was crazy! God answered by miraculously striking the altar that Elijah had prepared. Suddenly fire fell from heaven burning the wood, the soil, the stones, and even the water he had poured on the altar. Elijah's God proved once again that He was the God of Israel. The people were stunned. God performed a complete turnaround. The false prophets were put to death, and rain fell on the drought-stricken land.

Wow! You talk about a miracle event. But even after God revealed His power, Ahab and Jezebel did not bow. Within two verses, they were breathing death threats to Elijah again. I guess that is not surprising. But what is a little hard to figure out is why Elijah responded as he did to their words:

> Elijah was afraid and ran for his life.
>
> —1 KINGS 19:3

Now wait a minute, you may be thinking. How could that have been a real problem? Running to protect yourself was probably a good idea since Elijah was clearly under threat. However, the emotion that proceeded the action of running makes us have to question the prophet's action: fear.

Fear is not an accurate motivator. In fact, fear can cause us to do some incredibly stupid things. Like the time many years ago when I bailed out of my vacation house in the middle of the night after watching a scary movie. I was imagining all kinds of dangers as I ran to my car to escape the house with the creaky noises.

Fear can make us look silly, cause us to make wrong decisions, and torture us with anxiety while we quake away in hiding. Surely that is why our God was so clear when He spoke "fear not" or its equivalent over one hundred times in the Bible! He knew that a mere man could not operate in confident faith and paralyzing fear at the same time.

This leads us to preparation number four: we must learn to conquer the spiritual force of fear. Please note exactly what I just said because in this phrase is the key to our preparation. The force of fear. For many years, I thought the ultimate sign of my spiritual maturity would be the conquering of all fear in my life. I was mistaken. No human being this side of heaven will be able to do that.

Fear can be understood as both a human emotion and a spiritual condition. The spiritual condition or force of fear is 100 percent defeated at the cross of Calvary. But the emotion of fear is intimately tied to our fallen human condition. It happens subconsciously before we even have a chance to respond.

Take for example, when I was walking on a country path recently and a snake slithered out in my view. Before I had time to think, I screamed and jumped backwards because the emotion of fear was well-conditioned in my mind. That reaction motivated by fear was probably not a bad thing at all. But what happened next was not at all helpful. I was paralyzed on the road. The emotion of fear had given way to the force of fear. Irrationally. The snake I was so afraid of was nowhere in sight.

Let's go back to our story of Elijah. We will not know for sure what God's will was for Elijah in that moment of threat. Maybe God was going to have him confront Jezebel in person. Maybe God was planning to strike her dead at the sound of Elijah's voice. We won't know because Elijah not only felt the emotion of fear, but he also gave way to the spiritual force of fear as well. How can I know? We will see what happened to him in the next preparation.

Fear is our enemy in this hour. We are at a pivotal time in our nation. We have threats coming against our Christian beliefs and a dark flood trying to take our families captive. We must be ready to hear God's voice and respond. One moment of fear could pull us off track.

Surely this is what Paul is explaining to the young minister Timothy when he said,

> For God has not given us a spirit of fear, but of power and love and a sound mind.
>
> —2 TIMOTHY 1:7 (NKJV)

Action Steps

We go to God's Word to build our faith. "Faith comes by hearing, and hearing through the word of Christ" (Rom. 10:17, ESV). A simple internet search of "fear in Bible" will yield you lists of helpful verses. The more we understand God's direction to "fear not," the more we will be motivated to learn to defeat it as an enemy to our lives.

Sometimes we can get accustomed to living from fear to fear or from stress to stress. Ask the Lord to show you if you have a fear habit that He yearns to break off your life.

1. Pray and repent if necessary if you have not obeyed His Word. When God says to "fear not" we must recognize that as the command voice. He is not making a mere suggestion for our personal peace and comfort. He is teaching us the ways of His Kingdom and exposing the ways of the dark kingdom.

2. Learn to distinguish between the emotion of fear and the spirit force of fear. You will have many opportunities to try that this week. As soon as you recognize the emotion of fear arising, stop. Refuse acting on the emotion of fear. Instead, pray a prayer something like this: Lord, what is Your direction in this moment? I refuse to give in to fear. I chose Your path of faith.

3. Learn to do hard things in faith... even while the emotion of fear is screaming in your ear! One of the best ways to defeat the force of fear is to ignore the emotion of fear and do what is needed anyway.

4. Surround yourself with testimonies of the the great saints who have faced their emotions of fears but refused to bow to the spirit of fear. Go to frontlinefamilies.org and click on this chapter's link for great resources to help.

5. Memorize 2 Timothy 1:7, and quote it whenever needed in a personalized way.

BANISH DISCOURAGEMENT

"Lisa," they would say shaking their heads and looking very sad, "we are so discouraged..."

Let's go back once again to our story of Elijah. We pick it up right where Elijah had been threatened by Jezebel, and fear got a grip on his heart.

> Elijah was afraid and ran for his life. When he came to Beersheba in Judah, he left his servant there, while he himself went a day's journey into the wilderness. He came to a broom bush, sat down under it and prayed that he might die. "I have had enough, LORD," he said. "Take my life; I am no better than my ancestors." Then he lay down under the tree and fell asleep.
>
> —1 KINGS 19:3–5

At that point God sent an angel two times to bring him food. After he was strengthened he got up and traveled forty days to Mt. Horeb, which is known as the mountain of God, and went into a cave to rest for the night. That is when the word of the Lord came to him twice asking him the same thing: "What are you doing here, Elijah?"

Isn't that an interesting question? It was if God was trying to get Elijah to own up to what God already knew. Maybe He wanted Elijah to come to terms with his own mental/emotional state.

Fear, discouragement, and depression were not God's plan! He was suffering in a weak human moment when the pressure of his circumstances and the force of fear caused him to move away from the Lord's voice.

I am comforted to know that even a hero of faith like Elijah can get into one of these miserable states. I am also comforted to know that while he was in his cave quaking and talking of dying, God sent a rescue effort to bring Him out! How often do we find ourselves in similar need?

Our purpose is not to just empathize with Elijah's fearful and discouraged state. We want to look at this story and learn. Even though modern science can tell us a great deal about depression as a physiological/mental state, it is only in God's Word that we discover another angle to its damaging nature. Depression is often born on the wings of discouragement, and discouragement is a spiritual force.

How do I know? Dissect the word: dis + courage.

The prefix *dis-* means "not," so this word is literally saying "no courage." It is odd because that is not how we usually associate this word. If someone turns in a prayer request at church saying, "Please pray for me. I lost my job, and I am so discouraged," we don't usually start praying for courage. We don't say: "God, I just pray for great courage for my sister. I pray she would courageously pick up the classified ads and tackle the job search with courage." Instead we usually say something like, "God, please comfort my sister in her time of trial. I pray you would lift her out of her pit of depression over this loss and help her to find a new job."

Hmm. I am wondering if we might get better results if we focused our prayers more for courage! This issue reminds us of the Bible account of what God told Joshua as he was beginning to lead the children of Israel into the Promised Land:

> Have I not commanded you? Be strong and courageous. Do not be afraid; do not be discouraged, for the LORD your God will be with you wherever you go.
>
> —JOSHUA 1:9

Notice how fear and discouragement are linked here. God is banishing both from the children of Israel. He is saying get rid of them both now! I have commanded you! I believe this verse helps clarify a spiritual principle we must grasp if we are to be the standard in this generation. It is simple but deeply profound: God is on the side of courage and faith.

The devil is on the side of discouragement and terror.

That is why in our world today we are living with the growing threats of terrorists in a climate of rampant depression and anxiety. Someone will need to resist this spiritual flood! Someone will need to expose what the enemy is doing, come out of the fleshly sensory realm, and draw near to the flood of power from God and grab courage.

Elijah fell into the trap of the spiritual warfare waged against his life. He bowed to the force of fear, fell into the trap of discouragement, and then sank into a pit of suicidal thoughts. He caved in (pun intended!). The same strategy is being used against us even now. Can you sense it all around us? We, unlike Elijah, can have the indwelling power of the Holy Spirit. We must prepare ourselves to resist the devil's tactic.

Action Steps

Here are some action steps for finding our courage:

1.   As usual, we must start with the Word of God. Courage is a matter of believing in the God who wins. Check out these verses: Deuteronomy 31:6–8; Psalms 27:14; 31:24; Proverbs 3:5–6; Mark 5:36; and 1 Corinthians 18:13.

2.   I am learning to build my courage. I am intentionally tackling the little events in life that I previously would shrink back from: the hard phone call I don't want to make, the appointment that I know will be hard. I am learning to march right in and *do today what I normally would procrastinate*. And I am finding the courage from God showing up!

3.   I have asked the Lord to make me sensitive to see the little traps of discouragement when they come my way. I have developed a spiritual discernment for this now as I am amazed how often that temptation is thrown into my path. Discouragement resisting is a lot easier than depression healing!

4.   Pray for those around you who are already discouraged. Ask God for an opportunity to teach them this truth. Many are suffering, thinking this problem is "all about them," and they do not know that discouragement is a spiritual warfare tactic. It does not even have to be tied to any particular event. It is in our collective spiritual climate. It must be resisted as any other form of temptation.

5.   I have canceled my own pity parties and learned to cry out to my God. He listens and cares, but He does not let me stay under the covers of despair.

6.   I am working to be a better encourager to those around me. It doesn't take much discernment to focus on problems and negativity. It does take discernment to apply 1 Thessalonians 5:11.

7.   When people are going through grief of loss, they are especially vulnerable to the spirit of discouragement. Pray for those who are grieving. Walk closely with them and let them know of your love and concern. Pray for courage for them (Ps. 30:5).

BEAT LONELINESS

Do you ever feel like you are the only one left serving the Lord? Maybe you feel as if everyone in your family or your workplace or your school has compromised in ways that you do not believe are correct. Maybe you even feel that way about your church friends.

In our last trip back to the story of Elijah from 1 Kings 19, we see Elijah felt the same way. Please note that it was the "I'm the only one" feeling that drove Elijah further off track. Let's go back to the events after Elijah had been fed miraculously by the angels and had travelled a distance to Mt. Horeb and hidden himself in a cave.

Once he got himself into the cave, God began talking to him. Remember, not just once, the Lord asked him the same question: "What are you doing here, Elijah?" (1 Kings 19:10).

And twice, not just once, Elijah responded with the same speech to God:

> I have been very zealous for the Lord God Almighty. The Israelites have rejected your covenant, torn down your altars, and put your prophets to the death with the sword. I am the only one left, and now they are trying to kill me too.

Wow. That was an honest conversation Elijah had with God. Elijah was desperate. He could see the reality of how backslidden and rebellious the people had grown. And he was quite sure he was the only guy left standing. I can relate to Elijah's sentiment, and I must confess that I have been guilty of similar talk. How about you? My talking to God sounded more like this:

> *God, do You not see how hard I am working to serve You? All these other people who say they are Christians have compromised or walked away, but I am still here, believing Your Word. This is really lonely, Lord. I don't know who to trust anymore. The nation is falling apart. I am so worried about that Supreme Court ruling, and there is no telling what is going to happen next. My children's peers have walked into darkness. It is terrible and so frightening.*

I think it is interesting that God drew that speech out of Elijah two different times. Perhaps God was wanting Elijah to hear the words flowing out of His own heart to face their full meaning. After a speech like that, one would wonder how God would respond. Interestingly, God did two things. First, He gave Elijah in verses 15–17 some very detailed words of instruction of where to go next and what to do next. That, of course, was very helpful. But after His final word of instruction in verse 17, God made a direct correction of Elijah's speech when He said:

> Yet I reserve seven thousand in Israel—all whose knees have not bowed down to Baal and whose mouths have not kissed him.
>
> —1 KINGS 19:18

He was, in essence, saying: "Elijah, you need to get up and get on moving toward the assignment I have for you. Follow My exact directions. I have always led you before. I will do it again. And as for thinking you are all alone, let's be clear about this. You are not as alone as you suppose. I have preserved My remnant that are known only to Me. There are actually 7,000 believers in this land who have not bowed to the false worship system. In fact, they have not even had an affection toward the false system."

I believe God is saying something very similar to us today: "My son or daughter, I am grateful you have stood as a prophet to your generation. Please know I will continue to direct your steps even as you see the world around you growing more hostile. You are not alone. I have preserved My remnant in your generation, and they are radically devoted to Me."

That is an awesome thought, is it not? God has a group reserved for Him. Romans 11 reiterates this same assurance. It is our New Testament second witness to this scriptural concept of remnant:

Don't you know what Scripture says in the passage about Elijah—how he appealed to God against Israel:

> Lord, they have killed your prophets and torn down your altars; I am the only one left, and they are trying to kill me? And what was God's answer to him? "I have reserved for myself seven thousand who have not bowed the knee to Baal." So too, at the present time there is a remnant chosen by grace.
>
> —ROMANS 11:3–5

I have often heard people ask: How big is the remnant in America today? And my answer to that question is, "I do not know." Only God can see into man's heart. Only He knows how many have been preserved from the dark flood. But the truth is, we are not alone—even if we find ourselves feeling alone.

Feeling alone can be dangerous for human beings. When human beings feel alone in a job, they face two hazards. First, the human emotion of loneliness can lead to the feelings of despondency and discouragement that Elijah felt. Loneliness can cause people to make poor choices because they want to end the negative emotions.

Another hazard I would term the "Lone Ranger syndrome." I am, of course, coining a phrase after the old-time cowboy show of the masked superhero who rescued people all by himself. We can get the same independent spirit going for us in the kingdom of God when we don't want to coordinate or collaborate or cooperate because we think "I am the only one left."

Both extreme reactions due to a feeling of aloneness can be overcome when we learn to rest our emotions upon the Lord and risk appropriate relationship with other believers. Pride says: "I can do this myself." Loneliness says: "I will do whatever it takes to not feel uncomfortable by myself."

Paul, in that New Testament discussion of remnant, adds a helpful revelation. He says, "So too, at the present time there is a remnant chosen by grace." He has chosen us! That is an awesome thought! His grace is what we need more of right now if we are to be His remnant. We are chosen by His grace, and we will be sustained by His grace. His grace is sufficient. His power is made perfect in our weakness (2 Cor. 12:9). We can even stand alone when necessary, because in reality we are never really alone!

Action Steps

Action steps to beat the problem of loneliness:

1.   Consider carefully your own personal attitude. Has resentment snuck into your heart or emotions? Are you "despising" the generation you have been born into? Do you often wish for another time or circumstance to be alive? Spend some time letting the Lord check your heart.

2.   Take stock of your own situation. Are you noticing a shrinkage in the number of your peers standing strong for the Lord? Take that concern to the Lord in prayer. Do you sometimes feel alone in your mission? What have you been doing with your feelings of "aloneness?"

3.   What do you think would be the Lord's criteria for identifying a modern-day believer who is truly a member of His remnant who had not bowed to the Baals or even kissed their face? Once you ponder those characteristics, ask yourself this question: "Am I a member of God's modern remnant?"

4.   How can you be a practical source of encouragement to those you know right now who are standing in the remnant of the Lord? How will you be a part of the solution...instead of the complaining problem?

5. As you are reading your Bible, learn to make mental note of those whom God called to stand for Him when others were turning away. Consider their lives and testimony. What can we learn from their example? Here are some key people to consider: Noah (Gen. 6); Daniel (Dan. 1:8); Elijah (1 Kings 18:22); Mary (Luke 1); John the Baptist (Mark 1); and Paul (2 Tim. 1:15).

6. Learn to pour out your heart honestly to the Lord, particularly in worship and prayer. Let Him hear your struggles. He will never turn you away! And once you pour out your pain to Him, perhaps He will bring you new direction and encouragement as He did our brother Elijah.

REDEFINE PERSECUTION IN OUR GENERATION

We are already under persecution. But most of us do not know it. When we hear the word *persecution* images pop into our mind, such as executioners in masks and bombs in churches. But what if the word *persecution* encompasses things that do not fit that stereotypical picture?

"Because of our relative inexperience, we Americans tend to have a limited view of persecution," says Paul Nyquist in his book *Prepare: Living in an Increasingly Hostile Culture.* "We typically think of it in physical terms (imprisonment, martyrdom), and as such, may question whether our experience truly qualifies as persecution. But this definition is too narrow. The biblical term suggests a broader view including aggression, oppression, and violence affecting body, mind and emotion.... Simply put, persecution is the societal marginalization of believers with a view of eliminating their voice of influence."[1]

In post-Christian America we will be learning more about persecution, like it or not. According to *Christianity Today*, while martyrdom did double in 2013 (to more than 2,100 deaths), most persecution is not violent. Instead it's a "squeeze" of Christians in five spheres of life: private, family, community, national, and church.[2]

Certainly I think most of us can relate to the squeeze!

It is time for us to redefine the concept of persecution for our generation. What if in America we do not need to have many barbaric killings to silence the Christians? Perhaps Christians here will shrink back, shut up, and sit down with a whole lot less threat than that! If we wait to label what we are experiencing as persecution until many people are killed, we could miss out on what the Bible teaches us to be doing. Many could fall away from the Lord under the pressure, including our children, our teens, our new converts, or our spiritually weak.

Let's list some of the things we are already experiencing in America that would fall under this revised definition of persecution. Things such as relationship estrangement, job loss or demotion, threats of removing children from homes, school pressures, name-calling, bullying, slander, online harassment, business-bashing, and generalized marginalization would fall under this category in addition to the occasional acts of violence. Just the threat of these can cause insecurity in our own hearts that causes us to let loose of God's Word.

Today I am following the cases of:

• Kim Davis, the county clerk who refused to issue wedding licenses to homosexual couples[3]
• A high school football coach who refused to give up voluntary prayer with his players[4]
• A 19-year career Navy chaplain who was told to refrain from praying in Jesus's name[5]

That is just today. These are people suffering persecution for the cause of Christ and are resisting being silenced.

Please do not hear me wrong. I am in no way suggesting that these pressures are at all comparable to what our brothers and sisters in many parts of the world are experiencing. But neither are they to be ignored or trivialized even if some media and liberal distracters try to claim they are non-existent.[6]

Just for the sake of example, let's imagine what sort of persecution could come my way for writing this book. I believe the odds of someone coming to my door with a weapon are quite low. (Thankfully, but still it is a risk.) As I have seen before, the persecution will take some or all of the following paths.

I will be accused of being a hater and a phobic of various sorts. I will be ridiculed. These accusations will come from online bloggers and book reviewers. Some will call me narrow-minded. Others will call me archaic and controlling. The more ambitious detractors will take the time to go into this book, lift out pieces and attack them using exaggeration and innuendo (Alinsky style). Others will just repost a few phrases that they pick up from someone else. Some will find every little area where they think I was slightly "off" in this book and build a big case with my own weaknesses. Others will look back in my past and find any person I have ever mentioned or talked about any time in my life and claim all their errors are mine as well. Someone may note that I did not finish my masters degree in the liberal seminary, therefore my lack of "academic credentials" means I cannot write on these matters. Others will claim I should not be writing because I am a woman, while others will claim I shouldn't be a woman.:) All of those discussions will be annoying but pretty much expected.

The comments that are more painful are the ones that claim I am not a real Christian and that actually I am hurting the cause of Christ since I am not "walking in love" and am "being divisive." Those hurt my heart even as I know they are untrue. And then, of course, I may face personal attacks with vague accusations about how my ideas are "abusive to my kids and wrecking their lives." They may claim that we are all brainwashed and dangerous. All this might play out in cyberspace or it might leak into other spheres of our ministry, causing cancelled speaking events, or in my personal life, affecting our finances or personal security.

So maybe I should just not finish this book. Or maybe I should tone it down "for safety's sake." Or maybe I should go back and check my doctrines and "progress" them (which in my case would be regressing because I already was progressive in the past).

Do you see what could happen to me? Remember what persecution is according to the definitions above: Social marginalization with the goal of removing the voice. Historically, people who were persecuted were thought to be crazy or dangerous to the state or the church. Maybe that is how people will see me.

We are already living in more persecution in America than I have ever personally experienced. We are already running to the edge of our own personal skill base. This should send us running for our Bibles. According to the New Testament, persecution is normal Christianity. It is not abnormal. "Everyone who wants to live a godly life in Christ Jesus will be persecuted" (2 Tim. 3:12). So we can recognize the reality that we are simply now experiencing what God labels as expected.

That does not mean that persecution for the sake of Christ is easy! The Bible never claims that. What it does claim is a place of blessing, strength, and comfort to those who endure to the end under pressure (Mt. 24:13).

Let me put this rather bluntly. I think most of us are frightened by persecution. We look at the Middle Eastern Christians and figure we are not able to match up. We are too soft, too wimpy, and too ill-prepared. So we choose to either worry about it, ignore it, or escape it. All three are lousy options.

Instead, it is time for us to build our faith. We need pastors and leaders helping us, but they may legitimately claim that sermons on suffering and persecution are not traditionally very popular in the United States! Not many Scripture memory verse plaques have been sold on Luke 6:22: "Blessed are you when people hate you and when they exclude you and revile you and spurn your name as evil, on account of the Son of Man!" (ESV). We could blame our leaders and Christian marketers for this, but I do not think that is very accurate. We, as Americans, have craved a positive, success-oriented gospel message and voted with our dollars and feet to get it!

Maybe it is time for us to grow up a bit? Maybe instead of continuing to feast on the milk of the Word that makes us "feel good," it is time for us to move on to the meat of the Word it is talked about in Hebrews 5:11–14. There is a time for the elementary teachings as outlined in Hebrews 6. After those foundations, God is expecting us to take up scriptures that challenge us to the core:

> Do not be surprised, brothers, that the world hates you.
>
> —1 JOHN 3:13, ESV

For it is better to suffer for doing good, if that should be God's will, than for doing evil.

—1 PETER 3:17, ESV

For the sake of Christ, then, I am content with weaknesses, insults, hardships, persecutions, and calamities. For when I am weak, then I am strong.

—2 CORINTHIANS 12:10, ESV

I just sat here and looked over a list of one hundred Scripture passages about persecution. What an amazing list! I was matured just reading it as I was reminded that my natural response would run counter to God's amazing principles. Nowhere in that list was any excusing of immature, fleshly responses or compromise.

For years we have prayed for revival of our land. History tells us that persecution is often the doorway to revival. Frank Page of the Southern Baptist Convention Executive Committee, in an interview with a house church leader, asked how the American church should pray for their Chinese brothers and sisters. The leader is quoted as responding, "Stop praying for persecution in China to end, for it is through persecution that the church has grown."

Page went on to say, "What astounding faith he demonstrated. My admiration of his faith was quickly tempered by what he [the house church leader] said next. 'In fact, we are praying that the American church might taste the same persecution, so revival would come to the American church like we have seen in China.'

"Once I recovered from the shock of such a disturbing yet profound statement, I thought about the irony. We in America keep praying for God to bless us, while persecuted Christians in other nations are praying God will dismantle our arrogance through suffering so that we will become the vibrant and significant blessing God made us to be."[7]

Surely it is time for us to pray.

> *Oh God, would You send revival to us once again! Your gospel is what we need, Lord. It is the power of God for salvation to all who would believe. Prepare us to endure persecution that others may know and experience your redemptive love! Amen.*

Here are some keys to redefining persecution for our generation that will allow us to find extra access to the Lord:

Action Steps

1. Recognize persecution in your life for what it is, and then run to God's Word for His help and power.

2. Read this incredible list of one hundred scriptures on persecution and let God's Word begin to mature you. Study and show yourself approved to handle the Word on suffering and persecution. Go to frontlinefamilies.org to access the list or search it out yourself.

3. Pray for those you know who are under persecution in their families or personal life. Recognize their suffering, and lend your support. They need to know they are not alone. Make public support of those who courageously take a stand.

4. Make the redefining of persecution a point of study in your home and your church. I highly recommend the book I referred to in the opening paragraph of this chapter titled Prepare.

5. Watch over your children and grandchildren with care. Recognize that their experience is far different than ours a few years ago. We must protect their young hearts and young faith any way possible as we disciple them to stand firm.

6. Practice not backing down by doing simple acts of resistance. Carry your Bible in public. Speak up even if you are afraid. Ask questions and be ready to respond to the dark flood.

7. Many leaders have advised Christians to prepare for acts of civil disobedience when we are asked to violate conscience or faith.[8] How will you, your family, and your church prepare for those type of challenges?

HOLD ON TO
SOUND DOCTRINE

Something is wrong when only 9 percent of adults and less than 1 percent of millenials have a true biblical worldview.[1]

—George Barna,
*Futurecast: What Today's Trends
Mean for Tomorrow's World*

In March 2012, Matthew Vines posted a video on YouTube suggesting that "being gay is not a sin," and that the Bible "does not condemn, loving, committed same-sex relationships." He spoke eloquently from the heart with poise, conviction, and vulnerability. The video quickly went viral.

Vines is a bright young man raised in a Christian home. At age 19, he left Harvard University after his third semester so that he could "come out" to his family and friends in Wichita. He knew that his father would not agree with the way he reconciled his sexuality with Scripture. So Vines sought to arm himself with biblical scholarship on the affirmation of same-sex relationships and strove to convince his family and church that they were wrong—that homosexuality is not a sin." [2]

Matthew Vine's book, *God and the Gay Christian: The Biblical Case in Support of Same Sex Relationships* gained attention at its publication in the spring of 2014. *Christianity Today*, reviewing the book at its release, reported, "His aim is not to present new information, but to synthesize gay-affirming arguments and make them accessible for a broader and younger audience. Vines does a good job fulfilling this goal. Unfortunately, his book consists of some logical and exegetical fallacies, and it does not address the shortcomings of the authors to whom it is most indebted. And although Vines professes a 'high view' of the Bible, he ultimately fails to apply uncomfortable biblical truths in a way that embraces a costly discipleship."[3]

God and the Gay Christian represents the trend in America of revising or progressing doctrine to fit the cultural narrative. Notice some of the key points in the review above. This young man had a moral dilemma related to his sexuality that did not fit his Bible. So he found others who shared his concern, updated the arguments that had been espoused by previous theologians, and then sold his reasoning back to a biblically illiterate generation as a "new discovery." Never mind that his exegesis was flawed or illogical.

History will record how we respond to the shifting doctrines in our generation. Will we have the courage to study and show ourselves approved (2 Tim. 2:15) like previous generations? Or will we be remembered as the generation that played video games, watched movies, and built doctrine on whatever song trended in the modern worship culture?

In a scholarly book titled *A Summary of Christian Doctrine*, Dr. Edward Koehler writes, "To be true, a doctrine does not need to agree with human reason, modern science, public opinion, etc. Instead, it must in all parts and points agree with the Word of God. Jesus says, 'Your word is truth' (John 17:17), and 'If you abide in My word...you shall know the truth' (John 8:31–32). In God's church nothing but God's Word shall be taught."[4]

I believe many of us are dissatisfied with shallow faith living. In fact, I believe the true remnant of the Lord will surprise the world with their passion to hold on to the faith of our fathers, stand firmly on the inerrancy of God's Word, and still tackle the issues of our modern world. Researcher Thomas Rainer confirmed this as he reported, "In recent years, however, I have noticed a remarkable—and welcomed—return by younger leaders to the fundamentals of the faith, basic theological education, and the deepening of doctrinal roots."[5]

He went on to describe the increased emphasis on theological education in the local church. That is good news! If we are to counter the dark flood we must be ready to wrestle with doctrines of heaven and hell, sin and judgement, law and grace, tolerance and truth, salvation and sanctification, freedom and holiness and all the other truths of God's Word.

We cannot be afraid of healthy discussions on these important issues. In fact, as Rainer alluded to, people may actually be more eager to talk about foundations of belief than we have given them credit for. But we must enter into these discussions with wisdom and caution. The dominant cultural view of tolerance says that "everyone's opinion is equal and valid." This fallacy infiltrating church small group discussions sometimes causes more doctrinal confusion among participants than clarity.

Let's take a peek into how American adults who identify as "born again believers" according to Barna research view areas of key doctrine:

- 46 percent believe in absolute moral truth
- 40 percent believe Satan is a real force, not symbolic
- 47 percent reject the notion of earning salvation through good deeds
- and less than 62 percent strongly believe Jesus as sinless[6]

Now remember, these are the beliefs of the "Christian" people, not the ex-Christians or the secularists! We clearly have a lot of confusion out there. We need leaders and teachers among us to help us learn foundational doctrines once again! Without the renewing of our minds to the core teachings of the Bible, we are helpless against compromise or full blown deception.

This brings us to a logical but sticky question. What should we do if we find ourselves surrounded by those who have turned from sound doctrines and are following unbiblical belief systems? Let's go back to Koehler's book for a clear statement on this issue:

> "It is the duty of every Christian to examine for himself whether the teachings of his church agree with the plain teachings of the Bible. (Acts 17:11; 1 John 4:1). We may not take another person's word for it. This

is a matter of personal conviction and personal responsibility. We do
not accept any doctrine on the authority of a professor or pastor, priest
or pope, or because a synod or a church council has so decreed. We do
so only because it is plainly taught in the Word of God: 'God's Word
shall establish articles of faith, and no one else, not even an angel can
do so (Galatians 1:8).'" [7]

It is our job to hold on to sound doctrine! It is also our job to recognize
false teachers and prophets who are introducing dangerous errors. Jesus exhorts
in Matthew 7:15, "Watch out for false prophets. They come to you in sheep's
clothing, but inwardly they are ferocious wolves. By their fruit you will recognize
them." Be ready to inspect the fruit from others' lives—not just the words they say.

Here are a few of the doctrinal questions of our day. Are you prepared to
recognize the truth from the error as regards to these issues? As you consider
these, perhaps you would add others to the list as well.

1.   Universal salvation or reconciliation
2.   Revisionism and the rejection of scriptural authority
3.   False teaching of grace
4.   Deification of man and man's systems
5.   Antinomianism (rejection of all law)
6.   Overemphasis on prosperity
7.   Rejection of hell
8.   Rejection of Jesus as the only way to God [8]

Action Steps

Are you prepared to recognize the false teachings of many of the newer Christian
movements in America? Are you well versed in sound doctrine yourself? Do
you have a Biblical worldview? Here are some helpful tips to reinforce sound
doctrine in your family and church:

1.   Go to your pastor and let him know of your eagerness to learn
     your church's doctrines and beliefs. Ask him for the doctrinal
     statement for your church and any study materials he would

recommend. (Be prepared for the shocked but excited look on his face. You can imagine this is not a common request!) Evaluate your doctrines in light of God's Word.

2.   Be extremely cautious of anyone who is claiming they have found a new doctrine that no one in 2000+ years of church history has ever known before. It is right to put the doctrine to the Scripture test but remember, by very definition, progressives do not believe that is how you determine doctrines. They believe doctrines change with the times. Take your questions to a trusted, mature believer. (A great resource to help with this is the book cited at the top of Chapter 10—*Distortion: How the New Christian Left Is Twisting the Gospel and Damaging the Faith*.)

3.   Learn the foundations of church history. Arianism and Gnosticism that plagued the early church are very similar to many of the "new doctrines" of our day. Go to frontlinefamilies.org for some great links to help.

4.   If you are not in a church that uses traditional liturgy on a regular basis, consider looking up the Apostle's Creed and the Nicene Creed and learning why those statements of faith were important corrections in the early church. Read some of the ancient hymns. Explore the *Book of Common Prayer* or some other books written at the time of the Reformation that shaped Protestant worship for hundreds of years. Read classic sermons by some of the great preachers, such as Martin Luther, Charles Spurgeon, Jonathan Edwards, John Wesley, Andrew Murray, or Charles Finney. I have been doing this more in the last year and found it a real blessing. In fact, I had the pleasure of recently discovering some old Bibles and prayer books that belonged to my great grandfather who was a Methodist pastor. His sermons and notes could have been written last week—they were so relevant! When we discover how our faith has stood the test of time, we gain confidence in the gospel holding in our generation as well.

5. Dive into the world of apologetics. Be ready to defend your faith using sound reason, scriptural backing, and historical confirmation. The body of Christ is well equipped with expert apologists. Men such as Lee Stroebel, Ravi Zacharias, Josh and Sean McDowell, and Frank Turek have books, videos, podcasts, phone apps, and websites waiting for you. Go to frontlinefamilies.org and get started for you and your family.

6. Enter into a discipleship program with another mature believer. Perhaps your church and your pastor already have a bible study/discipleship program waiting for you. If not, start your own self study program using a quality discipleship resource. We have suggestions on our website.

7. *Read the Bible over and over again!* Listen to Scripture over and over again. This is surely the *best* way to grow in sound doctrine.

8. Learn to distinguish cults and false religions. If you have never studied the characteristics of false teachers and false churches, now is the time to do so!

9. Consider studying a time-tested theology textbook from a conservative Christian author. Your pastor may have a good suggestion.

10. Study in your family these six doctrinal views used to define a Biblical worldview by Barna Research. Be ready to defend these doctrines against modern heresies.[9]

    • Absolute moral truth exists.
    • The Bible is totally accurate in all of the principles it teaches.
    • Satan is a real being or force, not merely symbolic.
    • People cannot earn their way into heaven by trying to be good or by doing good works.
    • Jesus lived a sinless life on earth.
    • God is the all-knowing, all-powerful creator of the world and still rules the universe today.

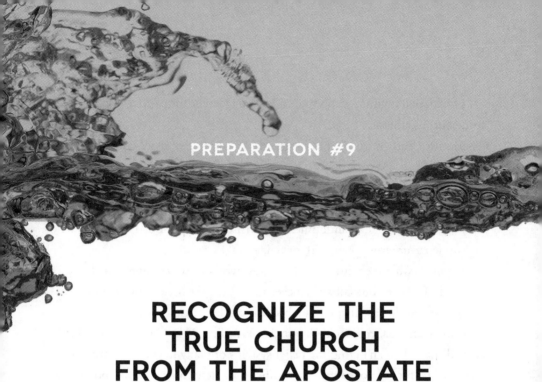

RECOGNIZE THE TRUE CHURCH FROM THE APOSTATE

We believe that each man must find the truth
that is right for him.
Reality will adapt accordingly.
The universe will readjust. History will alter.
We believe that there is no absolute truth
excepting the truth that there is no absolute truth.

We believe in the rejection of creeds,
And the flowering of individual thought.

—Steve Turner,
Known as the Creed of the Modern Thinker[1]

Who ever heard of something called an atheist pastor? How can you have a pastor who is not a believer? This idea seems to be an oxymoron, but unfortunately it is a reality in modern day America. Infamous atheist Richard Dawkins helped launch an organization in 2011 called The Clergy Project that provides anonymous support and encouragement for pastors who want to "come out" as atheists.[2]

Scripture clearly warns that in the last days a counterfeit representation of the church will arise and trick many people. Second Thessalonians 2 uses the Greek word *apostasia*[3] for the falling away that will happen as the secret power of lawlessness rises in the spirit of the antichrist. Apostasy, according to Webster's 1828 dictionary, is "an abandonment of what one has professed; a total desertion, or departure from one's faith or religion."[4]

Apostate is what Hebrews 6 labels as those who were once enlightened to the Lord and His Word but fall away never to be brought back again. Heresies, as we discussed in the last chapter, unchecked, can lead to apostasy.

Dannett and LaScola in their article "Preachers Who Are Not Believers" revealed that when analyzing the belief systems of many liberal denominations who have embraced tolerance, it is difficult to determine at what point the beliefs would no longer be defined as Christian.[5]

So if this is a problem among some clergy would it also affect others in the church pew? Recent research would indicate yes. One of the greatest demographic shifts noticed in religious views of Americans is called the category of the "nones"—those who self-identify as atheist, agnostic, or nothing.[6]

In 2014, 23 percent of all American adults bore the "none" label which is up from 16 percent in 2007. One of the greatest shifts in that study was among millennial young adults. More than one in three of them self-identified as nones. "For every person who has joined a religion after having been raised unaffiliated, there are more than four people who have become religious "nones" after having been raised in some religion. This 1:4 ratio is an important factor in the growth of the unaffiliated population."[7]

This, of course, is quite alarming to parents and leaders.

So we see at least three issues to note: The rise of the organized heretical or apostate church, the slipping away of those whom at one point identified as Christian, and the confusion to know the difference. As we consider the rise of persecution in our nation with the goal of the silencing of biblical Christian influence, perhaps we should also be aware of another risk. Over history when pressure comes on the church sometimes the heretical or apostate version of the church becomes the one recognized or blessed or "allowed" by the government while the true biblical church becomes increasingly marginalized and perse-cuted. Think of the difference between the state sanctioned church in China and the underground church. Do we have this type of "church split" happening now in America due to the issue of homosexuality?

Martin Luther in the days of the Protestant Reformation wrote a great deal about what he termed the visible and the invisible church. He was looking to differentiate between the official ecclesiastical group of people who call them-selves the church from those who are known and marked by God as part of the Body of Christ as His true church.[8]

Obviously only God can know the condition of man's heart. But we do know that many who think they are in the church will be surprised at the final judge-ment (Mt. 7). Knowing this should cause alertness in our lives.

It is highly unlikely someone will just one day deny their faith and turn apos-tate. Generally heretical doctrines infiltrate the mind, will, and emotions first. So how do we protect ourselves from these destructive forces? Learning to align ourselves with the true invisible church that will persevere until Jesus comes again and takes His bride to heaven must be our passion.

I believe God is preserving His true church in this hour from apostasy. I also believe God has true believers in many different denominations and expressions of His body. We should strive for unity in the body of Christ allowing some room for one another on "non-essential doctrines" in accordance with Romans 14. (Of course, over the ages, many have argued as to what is essential and non-essential.) We truly need each other—especially as we are experiencing the dark flood (Romans 12). Perhaps the growing pressures will cause us to finally figure this out!

Let's pray together...

> *Oh God, there is a great cloud of witnesses who is cheering us on.*
> *Help us, Lord, to maintain faithfulness to your Body, the true church.*
> *Open our eyes and cause us to come out of the false and into the true.*
> *Help us walk in truth and unity in this vital hour. Amen.*

Tips for Recognizing the True Church From the False

1. Read the Book of 1 Corinthians. Paul was correcting the church in Corinth which many would consider very similar to the American

church today. Then go to Revelation 1–3. Notice the sharp correction the Lord gives to the seven churches and apply them to your own life.

2. Pray for an ability to discern light from darkness. (See Philippians 1:9–11.)

3. Commit your heart to reading and/or listening through the New Testament several times this year. Some of my greatest times of sharpening my own ability to discern truth from error in my everyday life have come during seasons when I was letting the Word wash over my mind. (See Romans 12:2.)

4. Read *Pilgrim's Progress* by John Bunyan, published in the 1600s. Its classic message has helped many generation of believers to recognize temptation and error. You can find links to other classic works on our website.

5. Read and study *Creed* by Steve Turner (also known as the Modern Thinker's Creed or the Atheist's Creed). This one-page poem exposes many of the challenging thought processes of our age. (Read this at frontlinefamilies.org.)

6. Learn to be like the Sons of Issachar. According to 1 Chronicles 12:32, they were "men who understood the times and knew what Israel should do—200 chiefs, with all their relatives under their command." We must be able to recognize the dominant characteristics of the six primary world views in our world today: Secular Humanism, Marxist-Leninism, Cosmic Humanism, Postmodernism, Islam, and Christianity.[9] Go to our website for links to training materials I have used to teach this. Every week I write a news brief to help believers understand the worldview by interpreting worldview issues. Sign up for the Project 7000 news at our site.

7. Intercede earnestly for your brothers and sisters in the Lord as Jesus did in John 17:20–23.

PRACTICE DISCERNMENT ONLINE

Discernment: noun. the power or faculty of the mind, by which it distinguishes one thing from another, as truth from falsehood, virtue from vice; acuteness of judgment; power of perceiving differences of things or ideas, and their relations and tendencies.[1]

We live in an incredibly unusual age where everyone can become famous, start their own media channel and become an overnight expert or celebrity. Learning to discern online is absolutely critical.

We have been inundated with information. Business marketers, ideological revolutionaries, and political leaders know what makes us tick. Promise us easy money, free goods or services, or freedom and many of us will follow you wherever you want us to go! We must learn to sharpen our thinking skills if we are to distinguish truth from falsehood. Right now I am making sure my own children are getting a good educational foundation in logic and critical thinking so they can recognize the fallacies in modern advertising and debate.

As committed Christians we are not only limited by what our mind has to offer for discerning truth. Jesus opened up for us the path of wisdom from the Lord. What we need is what the New Testament calls *diakrisis*.[2]

According to Vine's Expository Dictionary *diakrisis* means "to make a distinction, to decide a dispute or make a judgment, or to discern or distinguish good from evil."[3]

Discernment should be the constant activity of the believer who is under the leadership of the Holy Spirit.

When I watch the online activity of many of my Christian friends, I am sincerely wondering about the level of discernment in the body of Christ. I see reposting of comments on Facebook from sources that are far from godly, Christian women's groups attending *50 Shades of Gray* movie openings, and the inclusion of far left political candidates quotes on Christian sites. What is going on?

The Bible makes it very clear how a Christian grows his or her own level of spiritual discernment. Discernment is closely tied to true wisdom which is freely given from our God. It is not a mystery. We will need to do just what the Bible says to acquire it:

1.   Ask for it in prayer. (James 1:5; Phil. 1:9–10)
2.   Distinguish it from earthly, carnal wisdom. (1 Cor. 1:18–31)
3.   Walk with the wise. (Prov. 13:20)
4.   Desire it and seek it. (Prov. 1)

Besides wisdom, discernment involves something of the spiritual realm that is spoken of in 1 John 4 as the testing of the spirits and in 1 Corinthians 12 as the discerning of spirits. Both scriptures help us understand that not all things that we see on the outside are as they appear on the inside. To distinguish the work of the demonic darkness involves the ability to see past the outside masquerade that 2 Corinthians 11:14 describes and into the spirit realm.

When we are practicing discernment online, we must be prepared to sort out the Christian beliefs of writers and websites. Below is a list of some of the newer movements within Christianity. This is not an exclusive list and, unfortunately, the definition of the terms are not uniform in usage. But never-the-less, a simple

Wikipedia level search on each term can be helpful in sorting out the names and players online. I just did that recently, and it was very informative. I recommend each of us take the effort to learn of these groups/ideologies.

This is especially important for young believers who may not know as much about the history of various people and ideas. For instance, a popular millennial blogger is Rachel Held Evans. Rachel used to be an evangelical Christian, but now she has moved her doctrine and would be labeled a progressive Christian.[4] Understanding an author's theology is critical. Often people will sprinkle these buzzwords in their bios on their sites.

Terms to know in 21st century American Christianity:

Progressive Christianity	Affirming Church
Moralistic Therapeutic Deism	Post-evangelicalism
Social Gospel	Social Justice Christians
Liberal Christianity	Postmodern Christian
Emergent Church	Evangelical Left
Liberation Theology	Progressive Evangelical
Christian Left	

Action Steps

Applying skills of spiritual discernment online takes commitment and know-how. Here are some suggestions to increase in this skill:

1. Follow the four spiritual steps for growing in wisdom as outlined above.

2. Recognize that every person or organization writing online has a bias, worldview, and spiritual connection.

3. Check out all your sources online by following the links backward. Read the about pages carefully, but don't just stop with a quick glance of how they describe themselves. Click on links and see who they are connected with. Many people online have multiple "faces." Sometimes one face is a front for another. I discovered

this recently by researching the personal blog of someone who was writing for a Christian blog site. When I got to their personal blog, it was obvious they were not a true believer as their site was filled with blasphemy and profanity!

4. Learn about the behaviors of internet trolls. According to *Psychology Today* an internet troll could be defined as "someone who comes into a discussion and posts comments designed to upset or disrupt the conversation. Often, in fact, it seems like there is no real purpose behind their comments except to upset everyone else involved. Trolls will lie, exaggerate, and offend to get a response."[5] But behind the sadist world of your common internet troll is a more strategic realm of trolls that the popular site called Net Lingo identifies as strategic or tactical who plan and coordinate their activities online in order to infiltrate a site or cause.[6] Christian ministries are attacked with these trolls.

5. Recognize that many "religious" or even "Christian" news services or blogs may feature multiple streams of theological thought and doctrine. This can be confusing. You may see a post on a site one day that is doctrinally and biblically sound and the next day see one that is way off course. Two such sites I know of are Patheos and Religion News Service.

6. Watch out for exposé writing. People who claim they have "investigated and found the heretic" are often out of balance in their methods. Gossip and hearsay are very easy on the web. *Do not believe everything you read.* Review the Alinsky rules as you consider what the motivation is behind communication techniques.

7. Learn to ask these important questions when you vet a source of your information:

    • Who are they?
    • What are their philosophies and biases?

- Do they demonstrate integrity and character consistently?
- Who are they associated with?
- Do they play fair with others?
- Where did they come from, and who backs them?
- Is there a profit motivation for their reporting?
- Do they have credentials to back up their claims?
- Do they repost or report on news not substantiated or verified?
- Do they use slander, gossip, or hearsay?
- Do they use Saul Alinsky or Nudge tactics?

8. Learn to listen to the "checks in your spirit." These are those not-so-easy-to-explain senses that the Lord will sometime give us to detect darkness that are only verified later when the darkness comes to light.

9. Recognize the truth of Matthew 7. You really will know a tree by the fruit. Do *not* ignore bad fruit and think it is inconsequential!

10. Avoid cynicism or despair. There are no perfect people, perfect churches, or perfect news sources. Sometimes we take the good and leave the bad for the Lord to deal with.

GET OVER "IT"

Offenses and strife. Wounds and separations. Emotional hurts and hang ups. Painful seasons in life can damage not only our relationships but also our souls. But let's be honest. What is going to happen to us when we face the extra stress of persecutions and pressures when our lives are already under heavy stress?

Please do not think me to be insensitive. I empathize with those who are broken or bruised. I have lived through some mighty rough seasons myself. However, as far as it is in our power, we must do all we can to find God's healing path and "get over the problem"—whatever that problem may be. Time is urgent. We cannot afford to stay stuck in our pain.

Learning to stand together in the body of Christ is very important. But how will we be able to stand together as a family or a church during times of increased opposition or suffering when we cannot stand together at a simple family dinner or church potluck because of old wounds and offenses?

If we need to forgive someone, let's do it now. If we need help with conflict resolution, let's get the help to resolve our issues. If we need to get help in healing past wounds, let's dive into the Lord's Word, and let Him touch those areas of pain.

It is interesting how new trauma can sometimes cause us to let go of old trauma and give us a fresh perspective. Siblings who have never gotten along may suddenly make peace with each other when they find out mom has cancer. Husband and wife who have always bickered about little petty differences somehow fall into each other's arms when their newborn baby dies. A congregation that was at the point of a church split suddenly pulls together when they get the news that their pastor is facing a life threatening diagnosis. What happened in each of these cases? The increased pressures led to attitude and perspective changes.

But sometimes extra pressures do just the opposite to relationships. Siblings may become further embittered over mom's death and spend the rest of their lives fighting over her estate. Young parents may end up in divorce court after failing to heal from the agony of burying their child. And the congregation may explode even as the pastor makes a health recovery.

Pressure and suffering bring out the best and also the worst in people as they reveal and amplify the foundations within a person, a marriage, a family, a church, or a nation. Whatever is in us is bound to come out under stress.

Several years ago my husband and I endured incredible heartache and pressure when our teenage daughter's life exploded. The multi-year battle for her soul and life was the greatest sustained season of pressure our family has ever encountered. We were so grateful to watch God perform His miracle in her life, however the long-term trauma had taken a toll on our marriage relationship. But, since our marriage relationship was founded on the rock of God and His Word, we successfully weathered the storm.

Proverbs 22:3 says, "The prudent see danger and take refuge, but the simple keep going and pay the penalty." Prudence is the ability to look into the future, assess danger, and then ask honestly "am I ready to make a wise response?" Some may feel that prudence is limited to such things as saving money for a rainy day or storing up supplies for natural disasters. It's not. Getting over the "it" in our lives may be the most prudent action of all.

Today's prudent Christian who is mindful of the dark flood should be willing to ask God three gut-honest questions:

- Lord, what do I need to "get over" in my life?
- Which of my relationships need to be strengthened *now*...even as we encounter the weight of persecutions and suffering?
- Who do I need to radically forgive and release from my past?

Growing up in the Lord requires moments of heartfelt transparency. He is gracious and kind to reveal our vulnerable areas. And I am absolutely convinced He doesn't just reveal. He also is willing to deliver and heal.

Action Steps to "Get Over It"

1. Study key scriptures on letting go of the past such as Hebrews 12:1–3; Philippians 3:12–14, 4:4–8.

2. Learn to live as if you were a Teflon nonstick coated pan, with nothing sticking on you and nothing dragging on you from behind. This has been one of my major growths in the last several years. It is not easy, but with the Lord's grace, we can rise above the painfully annoying issues of life. I am learning to let others have their emotional fits while I just stand by, watch, and pray for them. Patiently. Lovingly. Waiting for them to come to their senses. Sometimes I just move on past their silly errors even when they don't seem to want to let go. We really do not have time for petty arguments. Our energy must be saved for real battle. Here are some great attitude adjusting scriptures to meditate on: Luke 23:34; 1 Peter 4:8; James 1:19; Matthew 18:22; James 3:13–4:3.

3. Get the help you need. Do not procrastinate or stay in a place of denial. Some of us are up against major life issues. Some may have complex issues related to abuse, addictions, or other difficult life struggles. Getting professional help may be the best investment of time, money, and energy you have ever made. Seek the Lord's plan for your recovery as a matter of priority and urgency.

4. Go to our website for links if you need help "getting over it."
    Check out our book *Unmask the Predators* for help in healing
    pain.

5. Read an incredible book titled *Envy: The Enemy Within* by Bob
    Sorge. It will convict and heal!

HOLD ON TO AMERICA

America was founded by people who believed that God was their Rock of safety. I recognize we must be cautious in claiming that God is on our side, but I think it's alright to keep asking if we're on His side.

—Ronald Reagan
40th U.S. President[1]

My daughters Rebekah and Hannah were in Europe when the Supreme Court decision *Obergefell v. Hodges* was handed down. They missed the rainbow lights on the White House and the intense celebrating on Supreme Court steps. But they didn't miss the aftermath.

As they were boarding their plane at the airport to come home, something unpleasant hit their hearts. "I felt embarrassed, Mom, to wave the little flag at the welcome back celebration," Rebekah explained to me when she called me at her landing. "For the first time in my life I felt ashamed of the land that I love."

I love my country, and my heart hurts just like Hannah's and Rebekah's. Though I am deeply disappointed with the recent changes to my country, I will not give up on the United States of America, and I will not deny the Godly legacy we were founded on! I am going to do my best to convince you not to give up either.

The final chapters of our nation's history have not yet been written. We are still actors on the stage that will become our children's and grandchildren's platform. If we give up and turn our backs on our nation right now, what will happen to their future freedoms?

I have been alive long enough to remember many of the political seasons of this great land. I remember the Moral Majority of the 1980s and the euphoria of the Reagan years. I remember the excitement of the Christian Coalition in the '90s, the massive mobilization of the vote in the early 2000s, and the devastating defeat of the Christian voting electorate in 2008. And as these seasons ebbed and flowed with all their corresponding drama, I remember the great calls to prayer by those who took 2 Chronicles 7:14 very seriously.

This brings us to today. What will our response be in the midst of the continual bad reports? Will we disengage from the political arena claiming the separation of religion and politics argument again?

I have read the reports that say millennials are leaving the church because they do not like the mix of evangelicalism and politics.[2] I have heard leaders debate whether we should therefore quit talking about helping Christians get elected into government places. But quite frankly, I cannot figure how that makes any sense.

Dr. Jerry Newcombe is a key archivist for the great D. James Kennedy Legacy Library. In his article titled "An Appeal to Christians Who Do Not Plan to Vote in November," he said, "I was asked to speak at our church recently, and the title was given to me: 'To vote or not to vote?' Are you serious? How can we not vote? We're in such a mess because we haven't been voting our values. I believe voting is imperative for the follower of Jesus. Jesus said that we are to render unto Caesar the things that are Caesar's and unto God the things that are God's (Mark 12:17). Surely, included in rendering unto Caesar the things that are Caesar's would include voting. In this country, which had such a godly foundation, we currently have the opportunity to vote our biblical values. But if we continue to lose our freedoms and fall prey to tyrannical power, ultimately, we will only have ourselves to blame.

"My long-time pastor, the late D. James Kennedy, PhD, said this about Christians and politics in general: "I remember twenty years ago, a Christian said to me, 'You don't really believe that Christians should get active in politics do you?' And I said, with tongue in cheek, 'Why, of course not, we ought to leave it to the atheists, otherwise, we wouldn't have anything to complain about. And we'd really rather complain than do something, wouldn't we?'"[3]

Jesus's response to living as a Jew under occupation of Rome can serve as an important model for us. Jesus participated in His civic duty yet also pointed out the errors of both the governmental and religious leaders.

There is no doubt our nation has made many serious errors over the years. But this berating of America and trashing of our concept of exceptionalism has been an untrue narrative pushed by the progressive agenda to cause us to let loose of our nation. Remember Sal Alinsky's tactics? What do we think would happen to a country that told its children over and over again that the nation is bad?

In our new post-Christian America we are told by many progressives that America is no more exceptional or special than other nations.[4] High schools have cancelled their America Celebration Days because of fears of offense,[5] universities teach classes that berate the nation,[6] and other schools ban clothing that bears the American flag (American freedom law center[7]).

Christians, we must understand that as we contribute to the "America bashing" we contribute to the narrative's force to cause our nation to fundamentally change course. Perhaps we should learn to apply the truth of James 3 and use our tongue to turn the rudder of our ship toward a mouth of blessing. Our children need to hear from us the strengths of our nation. All they may be hearing is "how bad we are."

I do not believe God is finished with our land. I believe the nation that has more people who identify as Christian than any other nation of the world should be defended (Pew Forum, May 12, 2015).

As I see it in Scripture, our responsibility before God is at least three-fold in regard to our country. We are to pray, vote, and participate. Our faithful stewardship over a nation that has been entrusted to the will of the people is both a moral and spiritual duty. We are never to worship our country or confuse our patriotism with biblical faith. But neither are we to ignore our responsibility to safeguard our children's future and preserve religious liberty so that all men may hear of Jesus Christ.

Action Steps

Here are some practical ways we can hold on to our nation:

1. Pray fervently, both in public and private.

2. Continue to teach our children and grandchildren truth about our godly heritage. As God has been removed from the public policies and public schools of our nation. History is often taught from a revisionist point of view. Go to frontlinefamilies.org for resources to help.

3. Register and vote in every election. Research the candidates. Recognize that none of the candidates will be a perfect selection. Pray and ask the Lord for wisdom to identify the choice that will most closely represent His Kingdom values.

4. Support those Christians who are running for office and working in our government for us. Recognize they are up against a massive battle. Pray for them, and encourage them often.

5. Participate in your government by contacting your elected officials. That is our system, and we need to use the system that was established to maintain our freedom.

6. Study the United States Constitution. It is an amazing document written by men seeking divine wisdom. We must be ready to defend it against attack. Look for helpful links on our website.

7. Speak words of encouragement over our nation. We all know we have many reasons to complain!

8. Participate boldly in the freedoms this nation was established on. If we do not use those freedoms, we can have those freedoms taken away. If you encounter religious discrimination, please speak up and even contact Christian legal teams as necessary. If we do not exercise our rights, those rights may very well disappear.

9. Give financially to Christian causes that are working to protect religious freedoms and Godly values. Sometimes we may not "like" the way some of those who are promoting religious liberties and Christian values are doing their work. Here is my thought. I really do not want their job...and so I am going to give them some room to do it their way! Sometimes we criticize bold people but we are not willing to jump into the arena ourselves. Let's learn to preserve the unity of the spirit in the bond of peace whenever possible (Eph. 4:3) with those who are on our team.

TAKE BACK THE RAINBOW

I have set my rainbow in the clouds, and it will be a sign of the covenant between me and the earth.

—Genesis 9:13

Gilbert Baker hijacked the rainbow symbol for his gay, lesbian, bisexual, transgender movement flag creation first displayed at a gay pride parade in San Francisco in June of 1978.[1]

How ironic that the symbol of covenant with God has become the symbol for the great attack against His Word and character.

In this chapter I am going to do two things. First, I am going to present a crash course on the history of the gay movement in our country. And second, I am going to encourage our next appropriate response.

Americans have radically changed their views on homosexuality and gay marriage over a short span of time. In as recently as 2001 Americans opposed same-sex marriage by a margin of 57 percent to 35 percent. In 2015 the statistics were nearly reversed with 55 percent supporting gay marriage and 39 percent opposed. That is a massive shift is due in large part to the massive shift of view within the youngest generation of Americans.[2]

Younger Americans have lived their whole lives in the middle of a propaganda war zone. For me, this became the easiest to understand when I began reading the history of the gay movement. Availing ourselves with the knowledge of what has happened is one of the most important ways to get us back out of the dangerous deceptions. Please refer back to our discussion on Sal Alinsky's *Rules for Radicals* as we look at a few key events that shaped our nation including:

1. 1969 Stonewall Riot: A violent conflict between a handful of New Yorkers and police that is heralded as the birth of the gay liberation movement. President Obama commemorates the 40 year anniversary of the event in 2009 by hosting gay activists at the White House and heralding Frank Kameny, an extreme sexual libertarian, as a hero.[3]

2. Homosexuality no longer labeled as mental illness: According to the American Psychiatric Association homosexuality was listed as a mental illness in the DSM-11, the standard Diagnostic manual, until 1974.[4]

3. Rise of Activist Groups: Many groups sprang up in the United States in the late '70s and '80s including the Human Rights Campaign (HRC), the National Gay and Lesbian Taskforce (NGLTF), the International Lesbian and Gay Association (ILGA), Lambda Legal, Parents, Families and Friends of Lesbians and Gays (PFLAG), The Gay and Lesbian Alliance Against Defamation (GLAAD), and the group that specifically targeted our schools called the Gay, Lesbian and Straight Education Network (GLSEN). Most of us are only marginally aware of these group's names. But we are all too aware of their massive efforts.[5]

4. A unifying strategy was initiated: A 1987 article by two Harvard graduate gay activists named Mark Kirk and Hunter Madsen offered a brilliant strategy that employed Alinsky-like techniques to further the gay cause. The title of their original article was

telling: "The Overhauling of Straight America." Their follow-up book was released in 1990, *After the Ball: How America Will Conquer Its Fear and Hatred of Gays in the 1990s*. Here is a direct quote from the book:

"...by conversion [toward public acceptance of homosexuality] we mean...conversion of the average American's emotions, mind, and will, through a planned psychological attack, in the form of propaganda fed to the nation via the media." "...our effect is achieved without reference to facts, logic, or proof."[6] Here is a summary of the book's plan:[7]

- Talk about gays and gayness as loudly and often as possible
- Portray gays as victims, not aggressive challengers
- Give homosexual protectors a "just" cause
- Make gays look good
- Make the victimizers look bad (using a psychological technique called jamming)
- Solicit funds (from corporate and foundation sources for the just cause)[8]
- Target young minds: The indoctrination of our children has been massive when we consider the changes in our public schools including: curriculum adjustments, sex education programs, policy changes, storybooks for young students, and homosexual groups formed on campuses such as the Gay Straight Alliance.[9]
- Discredit and vilify Christians: A common tactic is to vilify Christians by claiming "the Bible approves of slavery, polygamy, incest, etc, in order to portray Christians as rank 'cherry-picking' hypocrites for selectively condemning the practice of homosexuality."[10]
- This was even done by President Obama in speeches to the American public.[11]

- The name calling of "hater," "bigot," "homophobe", etc. plays into what is called the jamming technique. And then there is the strategy to use Christian websites to psychologically attack Christians in the comment sections.[12]

This is a very simplified and brief overview, but I think we can catch a glimpse of the process. No wonder our people have changed their minds in such numbers. That brings us to the next obvious question. What do we do now?

Action Steps

Here are suggestions for how we can take back the rainbow and live Biblical lives in the face of the massive change:

1.   Recognize that God loves all people. He is no respecter of persons. His heart is for all those who are struggling with same sex attraction and gender issues.

2.   Love deeply. Never are we to counter evil with evil, hatred with hatred, or dishonesty with dishonesty. Study scriptures including Luke 6:27–36. Repent of wrong attitudes and behaviors as the Lord would convict your heart.

3.   Build a thorough Biblical understanding of homosexuality. Do not let the popular press define what you and your family believe. Go to God's Word yourself. Particularly study Romans 1. Go to our website for help with Scripture studies.

4.   Invest the effort to study these issues further. Dr. Michael Brown has written three books I recommend. *A Queer Thing Happened to America* documents thoroughly the history of what has happened to us. *Can You Be Gay and Christian?* outlines the biblical argument against the modern revision of Scripture by the Progressive Christian movement. And *Outlasting the Gay Revolution: Where Homosexual Activism Is Really Going and How to Turn the Tide*

offers hope to those of us who will continue to stand on biblical principles. I love Dr. Brown's eight keys for Christians to outlast the anarchy of the gay agenda.

5. After you become well informed yourself, *please* talk to your children, grandchildren, parishioners, and peers. Without sensitive and truthful conversation and ongoing debriefing, few will be able to stand against the propaganda.

6. Pray. We must consider this battle for what it really is: a battle for the souls of a nation.

7. Read the testimonies of those whom God delivered out of homosexuality and transgender issues. I highly recommend Dennis Jernigan's testimony of coming out of homosexuality and Linda Seiler's testimony of being set free of transgender issues. Information on their resources can be found on our website.

8. So many good Christian people have been impacted by this issue. Be ready to recommend helpful organizations that can minister to broken and wounded hearts. You can find links at frontline-families.org.

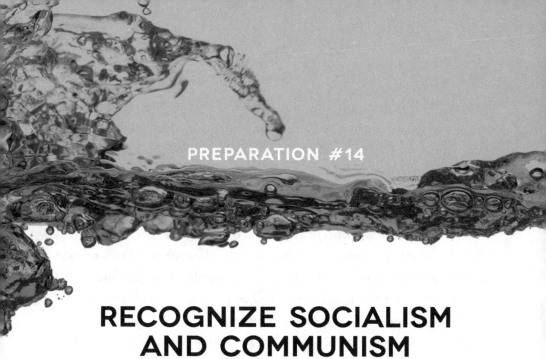

RECOGNIZE SOCIALISM AND COMMUNISM

In liberal Protestant circles—today rebadged as 'progressive Christianity'—the mythic elements of the Bible are dismissed as not historical and therefore untrue, leaving only Jesus the social worker. A secular Jesus for a secular age.

—Rachael Kohn[1]

We talked about the dangers of capitalism and how to shift the world's wealth from the haves to the have nots. I was taught that big businesses were bad and social programs were good. We worked our theology around liberating minorities and righting social inequalities. And I remember being angry at conservative Christians who in our minds "just did not get it." Those were my days in my young adulthood when I attended a liberal seminary in pursuit of my Masters of Divinity.

Please do not view me as a former Jesus hater. I was not. I loved Jesus, but I was an intelligent young woman who had rewritten her Bible to fit the modern cultural narrative. I was studying the social gospel with a mix of liberation theology. Which, in case you do not know those terms, are the same basic elements of today's Progressive Christianity movement. Truly nothing is new under the sun even though each generation wants to brand the "new discovery" with their own terms.

(The story of how I came out of my liberal views to where I am now is quite interesting. You can read more about it in my book *Not Open*.)

I want to make myself perfectly clear. I was deceived. And that is why I am so passionate to make sure others today do not follow the same path I took because they have a heart of compassion but are not grounded in understanding the ideas they are espousing. It is time we unashamedly ask tough questions before it is too late for another generation of Christians.

Here is the big one: Are those who are involved in the social gospel getting their doctrine from the society or the gospel? As a person who was completely deceived by this ideology, I can tell you that in order to make my social gospel theology work, I had to alter 2,000 years of interpretation of Biblical teaching. I now know that the foundation of my beliefs were the tenets of progressivism, not historical, orthodox, biblical Christianity. The Bible was a series of myths to me. My faith was evolving (progressing) to fit the cultural narrative. I did not believe in absolutes, and I advocated a style of inclusiveness that was extreme.

It is beyond the scope of this book to provide a thorough discussion on these complex issues. However, I propose that a thorough analysis of these issues will be necessary to the modern Christian because of the dark flood and the infiltration of its political and economic ideologies into the twenty-first century church.

How we view issues of wealth, poverty, business, and government will be influenced by our reading of Scripture as well as our cultural experiences and narratives. Jesus was a man of compassion. He cared about the poor, the downtrodden, and the suffering. The New Testament charges the church to do the same. However, the social gospel and the Progressive Christianity movements are merging the call of Christ with social reordering.[2] Many are interpreting the gospel through the lens of social issues instead of vice versa.

Watch your Facebook feed for conversations among young Christians. Listen to the discussions, and you will hear the mixture of ideas. In 2013 Pew Research discovered that only 50 percent of Americans have a positive view of capitalism.[3]

Do you find this rather confusing? What are we really talking about here? What kind of change are we looking for as a culture and a church?

During the 2016 presidential primary race the far left democratic socialist presidential candidate Bernie Sanders spoke at Liberty University to a group of Christian students. As I read the news reports on the event I listened carefully for the young adults' response to his socialistic ideologies. *The New York Times* reported, "Most students who were questioned afterward said that their minds had not been changed about Mr. Sanders." However another section of that news report caught my attention when it said, "but Mr. Sanders did appear to change the minds of a few students."

"I liked almost everything he said," said Sarah Fleet, a sophomore who grew up just a few miles from the university in southern Virginia. She noted that she did not agree with Mr. Sanders' views on abortion, but that his calls to help address childhood poverty and hunger resonated. And there's no one who should be expecting everyone to agree on everything," she said.[4]

Wow. That young woman could have been me those thirty years ago. She wanted to help. She had a heart of compassion. But she did not really understand what Mr. Sanders was proposing and how Mr. Sanders's ideas have played out in history. Her desires to help hurting people if not addressed by the church could lead her easily into the new progressive Christian cause.

As I was pondering that thought, I ran across a post by a Facebook friend. She had obviously also read about Mr. Sanders's new-found popularity. Narcisa's words shook me to the core. (I will warn you. She is speaking very forthrightly!)

> This morning I feel challenged by some Bernie Sanders' sympathizers and by one of my friends who suggested it's time for me to share my story again. For those who have been toying with the idea of socialism, you don't know what you're doing. In our days communism comes disguised in socialism, because it doesn't look so harsh and it has been embraced by so many western industrialized countries. But let me tell you, before you play with this idea any further, it's time for you to study some history. The history that this generation has forgotten or doesn't even know about it... Wake up!
>
> I was born and lived under communism almost half of my life. Let me tell you how it was: first they come in and take away every book and

person that is a threat to the system. Then they will take your houses away and shuffle people throughout the country so you are destabilized and away from family. Everything goes to export, and the elite pockets the money while the rest of the country is left hungry with just enough to survive, no cars or gas, everything is bland and gray . . . they systematically cut your heat in the winter and hot water and electricity at night for the sake of "savings," but the truth is they want to break your spirit. There will be big pictures everywhere with the new dictator who will have no faults and will be worshipped in schools by your own children through songs and poems. The history will be rewritten, and everybody will live in fear, willing even to become informants for the sake of some puny favor or minor promotion or just to cover their back and be "safe." But believe me, nobody will be safe anymore. And by the way, communism goes hand-in-hand with Islam. So, the list goes on . . .

I'm one of the dinosaurs of this society, soon to be extinct, because I'm willing to remember and share what others have buried into their own memory due to pain."

Wow. I realized that many young minds might dismiss her words as extreme or inflammatory. They will cling to the idea that socialism and communistic dictatorship are not related and that they certainly would never happen in America. That is what I used to argue. But my Facebook friend is exactly correct. I argued that position out of ignorance of world history or of economic facts. I truly believed "everything should be free." The government, in my mind, was the solution with the gospel as the liberator.

If America is to survive as a land of freedom for all, we will have no choice but to address these issues in the church even when they are uncomfortable. If the next generation is to come to a saving knowledge of Jesus, they must sort out the truth of God's Word from the indoctrination that portrays lies as facts for the purpose of fundamentally changing our nation and then renames them as the cause of Christ!

I have great hope for this issue. I am a woman who changed her mind very quickly when the light of the truth of God's Word penetrated my soul. What God did for me, He can do for others.

Ultimately, this is a spiritual battle for the souls and minds of a nation. Thank God some people were courageous enough to confront me in my well-meaning deceptions. I will be eternally grateful not only to their words but also to their prayers that pulled me out of the darkness that held me captive.

The devil is a master at using these issues of social justice to drive a wedge between the generations. Here is what he is ultimately after: the passing of authentic biblical faith from one generation to another. How convenient for Him when people walk away from authentic faith in Christ to follow a false Christ. All while people are still in church!

We must be wiser than the devil's worn out plan.

Action Steps

Here are some tips to help us with this controversial issue:

1. Recognize that not everyone who is for big government programs is wanting a communist society. Obviously that is a divisive thought. However, we must recognize that very few people have studied these issues. Many will speak passionately as I did about that which they are ignorant about.

2. Make the effort to study the issues of socialism and capitalism yourself. Do not fall into the trap of hearsay and emotionalism. Put the issues before the Lord and ask Him to help you learn what you need to know. Go to frontlinefamilies.org for helpful resources and links.

3. Talk to someone in the older generation who remembers World War II. Ask them their perspectives on this issue. These people are a treasure to our nation in this hour. I did that recently. It was very enlightening.

4. Study the history of what happens to the church when various forms of socialism and communism are at work. Check out links at our website, or do a little digging yourself. Ask yourself: Why

did our Founding Fathers design our nation the way they did? Why do we want to change what they initiated, and who will ultimately benefit from these changes?

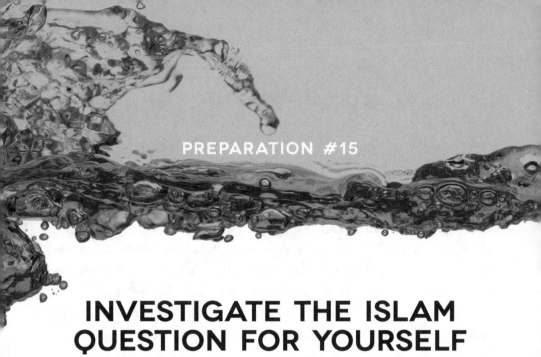

INVESTIGATE THE ISLAM QUESTION FOR YOURSELF

In Islam, they are awaiting the caliphate which is the form of Islamic government that will rule the entire world by the caliph, the holy Islamic leader. This is their end-times, world-domination doctrine.[1, 2]

In Christianity we are awaiting the second coming of our Lord Jesus Christ. His return will signal the end of this age and the beginning of the next.

In Islam, ISIS "declared the caliphate" in June 2014. And the world has been engaged in the massive aftermath of Islamic extremism attempting to enforce their declaration ever since.[3, 4]

In Christianity, many believe we are getting much closer to the Lord's return, which is called the End Times.

Many Americans seem remarkably unable to comprehend the truth about Islam and its threat to our nation and to the church. Perhaps many are ignorant of the Quran and of world history, or perhaps we have been taken captive by the modern rhetoric on the issue and need help looking deeper. While we are trying to figure it out, the radical groups are pressing toward their end-times domination plan.

I have encountered Christians who think Islam is simply another way to get to our God. That is preposterous. Islam is a religious, worldview, political system. It is incompatible with the Bible and completely opposed to the ways of Jesus. That is not just Lisa's opinion. It has been the truth since the times of Muhammad.

Just down the street from our church is a mosque. Over the last few years Islam has grown in prominence in our community. When the mosque was built, the leaders chose a location in the heart of our African-American community for a reason. The Muslims began targeting young men from our community as converts. Just recently a young mother who was estranged from her husband after his conversion to Islam came to our church. She did not agree with his religion, but she was totally unprepared to defend her faith and understand his deception. If we are to help our children and our fellow Christians resist the deceptions of our modern age, we must take the time and effort to understand the truth about Islam.

During the 2016 presidential campaign the question was debated as to whether it would be wise for Americans to elect an Islamic president.[5] The discussion in the media concerning the question revealed the inconsistencies in logic regarding the issues.[6]

For instance, to imply that "Islamophobia" is a racial issue is absurd.[7] Islam is not a race. Perhaps people are confused because the word *Jew* represents both a race and a religious group. But Islam is clearly different. Muslims worldwide are of various racial and ethnic groups. Think about it. Somehow the progressive agenda in America has mysteriously linked both gay issues and Islam issues to "racism." That makes no sense until we go back and study the *10 Rules for Radicals* of Sal Alinsky and notice how the debates and emotions have been manipulated!

When we see people who are pro-homosexual rights also screaming Islamophobia we should take note. In Muslim nations today homosexuals are sentenced to death in accordance with the Quran.[8] When we see strong feminists also advocating for Islam we should question the connection. The Quran says that women are property, and Muslim nations have very restrictive rules for women.[9] Clearly something very odd is happening here!

It is beyond the scope of this book to teach all the principles of Islam. But it is not beyond the scope of this book to recommend that Christians do their own research into this important issue. Our children in public schools of America are being taught a sanitized version of the Islamic story.[10] Our media is quick to expose any suspected evidences of "Muslim persecution" but fails to report evidences of Christian persecution.[11] Our presidents, both George W. Bush and Barack Obama have made shocking statements about Islam. We looked at President Bush's statement previously. Here is a statement by President Obama:

> And throughout history, Islam has demonstrated through words and deeds the possibilities of religious tolerance and racial equality....I consider it my responsibility as President of the United States to fight against negative stereotypes of Islam wherever they appear.

> —BARACK OBAMA
> REMARKS AT CAIRO UNIVERSITY, JUNE 4, 2009[12]

How will we in the church respond to the growth of Islam in the western world? That remains one of the hottest questions of the hour as we note the massive changes in our culture when Islam doubled from 0.4 percent to 0.9 percent between 2007 and 2014.[13] Undoubtedly, there are large percentages of Muslims both in the United States and worldwide who are peaceful, kind people. However a religious worldview belief system cannot be analyzed on personality traits of people but on doctrine, practice, and history.

Last week a woman visited our church. She was born into a Nigerian Muslim family. When she was eleven- and twelve-years-old, Jesus appeared to her in her dreams. She had never known anything about the Lord, and all of her relatives were Muslim. After two years of dreams, she snuck into a church and encountered our risen Lord! Since her conversion, most of her family members have come to Christ.

Her story was a fresh reminder to me of this simple fact: all the discussions about Islam and Christianity are really about one thing. Souls. Islam takes people captive to hell just as quickly as every other false belief system. As we are living cross-cultural as missionaries in our nation, we must be ready to understand the false religions confusing our people. Their eternities are at stake.

Action Steps

1. In studying the core teachings of Islam, find trustworthy resources. Many online sources of information write about Islam either through an Islamic point of view, of an Americanized *coexist* view. We need to look at Islam through a Biblical worldview.

2. In order to have a working knowledge of Islam we must understand many terms including: Islam, Muslim, Shariah law, the 5 Pillars, House of War and House of Peace, Hadith, Quran, jihad, caliphate, infidel, mosque, imam, Allah, and Mohammad. Reading parts of the Quran for yourself is very helpful. Go to frontlinefamilies.org for a list of helpful resources on historical Islam as well as contemporary Islamic issues.

3. Be willing to learn from those who are knowledgeable at witnessing to Muslims. This is one of the most effective ways to learn a cross-cultural comparison between Christianity and Islam.

4. Pray for our government leaders. Pray for truth to prevail and leaders to make wise decisions.

5. If you are a leader in your church, make sure your congregation has an opportunity to learn about Islam.

6. Be ready to counter the accusation that you are "Islamophobic." That term is used to intimidate. Lovingly and truthfully engage in conversation with others on these issues for the sake of allowing your light to shine.

7. Prison is a frequent path of conversion to Islam in America by African-American males.[14] What implications does this have to the church? Perhaps it is time to strengthen our prison ministries with resources, manpower, and prayer!

DEBRIEF YOUR TEAM

Fourteen-year-old Tyler returned home from a tough day at school. His health teacher had assigned the class a two-page research report that made Tyler very uncomfortable. He knew his parents would not want him reading the articles that would be necessary to fulfill his instructor's instructions. And in his own heart, he did not believe this was an assignment that honored his Lord. As he had gone up after the class to talk to his teacher about the assignment, two of his classmates overheard his discussion. Scoffing at Tyler, they both made it clear how ridiculous his concerns were and how much the rest of the class would enjoy hearing about Tyler's silly embarrassment.

Mary, a nurse at the local hospital, returned home, worn out from a day of confusing emotions. Her morning had started out wonderfully with a delivery of a healthy baby to a family who had been waiting for years for their first child. But the afternoon ended in torture when another mother came into the maternity ward screaming obscenities and refusing her care. It seemed this mother was unhappy to have been pregnant and had taken some drugs that she thought would cause her to abort her child. The abortion had not worked, and it was clear she was furious at the pain and inconvenience.

Pastor John also arrived home after a crazy day. A couple had come by the church looking for spiritual help and advice. They wanted to get married and had heard that Pastor John was the man in town who would help them after some of the other pastors had turned them away. But Pastor John was not able to give the two women what they had wanted. He told them of God's love and mercy, but they left the church furious and complaining about his "lack of love."

What did all three of these people have in common when they arrived home at the end of their day? They were in desperate need of personal support. Think of it like this. Each day Christians "fly a mission for Jesus." Each day they lay their hearts out in service to Him while keenly aware of the dark flood of resistance that meets them. They find themselves challenged to decode what is going on around them and live honorably before their King. Some may even be culture-shocked or injured by the people they are eagerly laboring to reach for Him. They need their ark of protection as described earlier.

As we live cross cultural in our new mission assignment, we know we must resist the urge to do what Elijah did and climb into a cave and pretend like we are the only people left standing for God. Isolation is not godly. Hardening of hearts and bottling of emotions is dangerous. Somehow we must identify our fellow mission team members and learn to support each other in practical and sustainable ways.

The healthy answer to this problem is something called debriefing.

Debriefing is an interesting word that is used most commonly in a couple of unique settings. One setting would be in a military unit, and the other setting would be on a mission field. Here is how a mission organization that specializes in supporting missionaries on the field explains the concept of debriefing:

> Debriefing is a biblical idea, practiced by Paul and the Antioch church (Acts 14:27), Peter (Acts 11:4ff), Tychicus (from Paul, Ephesians 6:21) and Timothy (from Paul, 1 Thessalonians 3:1–6), among others. It is an experience we have seen practiced with great benefit in Wycliffe and SIL International.
>
> Debriefing is more than giving a report. It is telling our story, complete with experiences and feelings, from our point of view. It is a verbal processing of past events. It differs from a report which is a factual sharing of details as objectively, accurately and free from

emotion as possible. Debriefing, on the other hand, includes both the facts and emotional responses, and invites feedback, including appraisal. Some elements necessary for good debriefing include relationship, responsibility, love, respect, concern, trust, and time. It is better if it is not hurried.[1]

Do you see what they are saying here? When people return from emotionally and spiritually stretching activities their souls need care to process the event. Without help, they are in danger of burning out due to the pressure. Debriefing is a form of active love that Doug and I have found to be extremely effective in our family and in our ministry. It works!

Just last week one of my sons encountered a very challenging experience. He discovered a longtime friend with whom he had shared his Christian faith, was now living with a woman in a lesbian relationship. He needed someone to talk to as he unpacked his emotions and his spiritual concern. That is why it was good he had already established a relationship with a team of people who would debrief with him after his experience. Doug and I have found this to be one of the most important keys to our family's success!

Christian homes are the best first line of debriefing support. But for many this is not working well. In fact, some believers may need debriefing help from their family stresses themselves! This is where the church must come alive to provide support to believers.

Action Steps

Here are some important keys for developing a debriefing lifestyle:

1. Take inventory today of all your God appointed ark-building teammates. Stop and pray for each one of them.

2. Purpose in your heart to begin to help others to debrief. Give the gift of active and heartfelt listening to others. Start with someone who is easiest to develop a relationship with. Show him or her this book and explain to them that you want to be there for them. Allow them to vent feelings and problem-solve challenges in an emotionally safe environment.

3. If you are a parent, small group leader, boss, or pastor, begin to ask the Lord for a strategy to help your people debrief often. Doug and I have determined that meals together and fellowship discussions where the leader dives into these sticky areas first is the best way to establish a debriefing climate.

4. Use texting or private social media as an avenue for people to sense they have a "lifeline of support" while they are in difficult situations. Sometimes people laugh at how many text messages travel between my family members in a given day. And I agree, some days the text beeping is intense! But what I am seeing is a group of people who are "doing life together" and debriefing as their day goes by whether it be lighthearted dialogue or heavier cries for prayer and help.

5. If you are a leader or mentor, learn to "think out loud" in front of your protégés. Take them in to your own personal world. Talk them through the tough experiences you encounter in a first person report. This is a highly effective way to teach others by example. Do not just share with them the facts about your life, but be willing, as appropriate, to share your conflicting emotions and pressures as well. As you talk, be sure you are not "dumping the weight on them." Show them how you turned your questions and weights over to the Lord and got back in to the beautiful stream of His presence. This, of course, will naturally cause you to run to the Lord more if you know you will be sharing your experiences with others. So that is a win-win!

6. Go to frontlinefamilies.org for some great links to help grow your skills.

RESTORE THE FAMILY ALTAR

When I mention the concept of a "family altar," perhaps you picture a little table decorated with a Bible and candles in a family's entry room or hallway. Actually, you would not be that far off of the historical use of the phrase. But that's not the image I am going for. I am talking about the establishment of a spiritual presence in your home where worship, prayer, and Bible reading are the norm. If we are to successfully be the standard of the Lord and step in to the flow of His flood of mercy and grace, we will need to open our homes to His presence in a new and tangible way. This is central to ark building.

My theory is that we know this—we just do not know how to accomplish this. We are too rushed, too busy, too uninterested, and too unqualified to have five minutes of family prayer time and Bible reading every day.

Hmmm. Don't we feel silly even trying to make that claim? Of course we could open our Bibles and pray together. If it was truly a priority and we thought it vital we would make a way.

But would a five minute religious activity be enough to truly shape our lives and build something in our families that would endure? We all know the answer to that. No, five minutes of dead religious ritual is not effective. But it is almost because we recognize that fact that we just end up doing nothing. That is pretty irrational, isn't it? Let's consider how to make it alive—not dead!

Throughout the history of our faith, Christians have recognized the vital importance of the family devotional life. It is silly to think that having a family alter is a novel idea rather than a necessity. The home has been a central place of worship and discipleship in many generations.

Let's consider what the leaders through the centuries have said about this issue:

- In the Old Testament: "Hear, O Israel: The LORD our God, the LORD is one. Love the LORD your God with all your heart and with all your soul and with all your strength. These commands that I give you today are to be upon your hearts. Impress them on your children. Talk about them when you sit at home and when you walk along the road, when you lie down and when you get up. Tie them as symbols on your hands and bind them on your foreheads. Write them on the doorframes of your houses and on your gates" (Deut. 6:4–9).

- In the New Testament: "Every day they continued to meet together in the temple courts. They broke bread in their homes and ate together with glad and sincere hearts" (Acts 2:46).

- Martin Luther, 1522: "Most certainly father and mother are apostles, bishops, and priests to their children, for it is they who make them acquainted with the gospel. In short, there is no greater or nobler authority on earth than that of parents over their children, for this authority is both spiritual and temporal. Whoever teaches the gospel to another is truly his apostle and bishop…how good and great is God's work and ordinance!"[1]

- *Luther's Small Catechism* has been used throughout the ages until modern times for teaching biblical doctrine in the home.[2]

- John Knox, 1557: "You are bishops and kings; your wife, children, servants, and family are your bishopric and charge. Of you it shall be required how carefully and diligently you have instructed them in God's true knowledge... And therefore I say, you must make them partakers in reading, exhorting, and in making common prayers, which I would in every house were used once a day at least."[3]

- Thomas Manton, 1646: in *Epistle to the Reader of the Westminster Confession of Faith and Larger and Shorter Catechisms* instructed families on daily worship.[4]

- Matthew Henry, 1704 sermon on family religion: "Masters of families, who preside in the other affairs of the house, must go before their households in the things of God. They must be as prophets, priests, and kings in their own families; and as such they must keep up family-doctrine, family-worship, and family-discipline..."[5]

- George Whitefield, during the First Great Awakening: "We must forever despair of seeing a primitive spirit of piety revived in the world until we are so happy as to see a revival of primitive family religion." He reiterated that "every governor of a family... [is] bound to instruct those under his charge in the knowledge of the Word of God."[6]

- Jonathan Edwards, 1750, "Farewell Sermon": "Family education and order are some of the chief means of grace. If these fail, all other means are likely to prove ineffectual."[7]

- Charles Spurgeon, 1908: "If we want to bring up a godly family, who shall be a seed to serve God when our heads are under the clods of the valley, let us seek to train them up in the fear of God by meeting together as a family for worship."[8]

- 1928 *Book of Common Prayer* used by Episcopalians and Anglicans and later adapted for Methodists, prayers included for household morning and evening prayers.[9]

So here is the question. How do we possibly think we can ignore what other generations found vital and effective?

Please do not hear me as saying this is easy. But after twenty-four years of successfully having a family worship time together in our home (by God's grace), I can testify that it is possible. I can also testify that it is necessary if you truly want to become a debriefing team that stands together in the midst of a dark flood. Our older children have told us as they have left our home how foundational our family devotional time was to their faith.

Each Christian home should become a house of prayer. It doesn't matter how many inhabitants are there. One, two or twelve. A house that learns to worship together will set roots that are not easily moved.

Action Steps

Here are some simple tips for reclaiming your family worship/altar:

1. Recognize that there will be resistance to a family worship time because it is a spiritual threat to the kingdom of darkness. Do not be intimidated when suddenly family members seem distracted or even hostile. Just press on in faith. Pray for your family and have patience and quiet resolve.

2. Start where you are. Start with a five-minute meeting once a week and build up. Just start!

3. Consider beginning with a short scripture reading and prayer over dinner.

4. Keep it simple. Family worship need not be complicated or laborious. Scripture reading, prayer, and worship music are the simplest elements to incorporate. Including personal testimony and debriefing style discussion helps build relationships.

5. Do not let the "we don't sing" thing hinder the process. Consider pulling up a worship song or hymn on your phone to listen to. Or skip music if you choose and use the Psalms. The Psalms read aloud have been the standard for worship for thousands of years.

6. Pray about the current needs in your home, your community, and the world.

7. Trade off the leadership role to keep things fresh and alive.

8. Five minutes gathered in a circle before work and school has power! Car meetings have power. Even virtual meetings on your phone can work.

9. Let this "family altar" gathering time be a chance to learn sound doctrine. Look at the previous suggestions. Perhaps Luther's short catechism or another type of tool would be of great help in your home. Check with a pastor or trusted spiritual mentor for suggestions.

10. Use the Nike slogan: Just Do It! We have many tools to help encourage you on our website.

RETIRE RIGID LISTS... LEAD BY THE SPIRIT

Six steps to a flat belly in ten days.
Fourteen steps to make your teen follow your rules.
Seven guaranteed ways to win at the stock market.
Eight rules that, when followed, will make your wife love you.

What is it about lists offered online that make me want to click on the articles? Online experts agree: traffic is much higher for articles that give a structured list. Perhaps it is because we all enjoy math so much that the numbers attract us in. But I doubt it. My theory is that people are like me. First, I believe I can skim read a list quicker. Second, magic bullet ideas make my hopes soar. Someone might have discovered the answer to my problem.

Sometimes a good set of rules or lists can be comforting. Checking things off the internal to-do list feels like we are accomplishing something important and soothes, at least for a few moments, our anxiety about things being okay.

When I was a new parent I yearned for someone to give me a rule book that I could follow that guaranteed me a healthy and successful child. I went to parenting meetings, read books, and listened earnestly for the perfect advice, and I did tap into some great plans that built my confidence as a young mom. After a few years, I naively thought I was ready to teach other moms all the wisdom. I could list out for them great ways to make things work. But then I had my third child and then my fourth. And by the time I had my fifth child I had re-written most of my lists!

That is when I learned that rigid rules are not all they are cracked up to be. So my most important "list of rules" about parenting was reduced to a new set of mothering criteria:

- Study God's Word.

- Grow up as a person yourself.

- Learn what you can from parenting experts' lists of advice recognizing that much of what they say that doesn't match up with number one on this list will change over time. (Kind of like the fashions in your clothes closet go out of style.)

- Retire an expectation of a quick fix to any human problem.

- Come out of a sprint mentality in parenting to adopt a marathon mentality

- Learn to listen to and obey the Holy Spirit because He always knows what to do!

There. You have my best advice after thirty-one years of professional leadership experience of parenting ten children. Perhaps it is so simple that we miss it while we are frantically looking for our next list of professional advice. What I learned in parenting, I find true in other arenas of leadership as well.

God refuses to be reduced to rules or formulas. He is far bigger and wiser than that! So instead of frantically seeking an answer to a question....my best advice is to seek Him and let Him bring the answer.

As we experience an increase in the dark flood around us, beware those who claim they can "fix our problems" with their lists. Marketing to fear will be very lucrative for some who are selling cheap answers. Anxiety and insecurity will cause us all to be tempted to grab on to the next trendy cure.

This is the time to develop our listening ear. If we are to be the generation that will live through the dark confusion of the end of the age, we know God will be speaking His words of instruction to His children. Those who have developed an ability to discern His voice will stay in His place of protection and provision fulfilling the calling for which He designed them. Others will panic, grab on to the false saviors, and fall for the counterfeit fix.

So here's what we can do now to develop our listening ear.

Action Steps for Listening to the Holy Spirit

My favorite section of Scripture about the Holy Spirit is surely John 14:15–16:16. I invite you to read that passage and let the Lord speak to your heart. Highlight it. Meditate on it. These are Jesus's words to His disciples so they would know how to be sensitive to the Lord's leadership after He went to heaven and they fell under pressure.

1.   These are great questions to take to your pastor and your spiritual mentors: How do you hear the voice of God in your life? What are some resources or tools you could suggest for me to help me learn to recognize and obey God's leadership in my life?

2.   The primary way God leads His children is through the Word of God. Developing and implementing a daily plan of Scripture reading and listening has always been the best way for me to hear God's voice.

3.   Reading the biographies of people of faith is very helpful. As I watch how others responded to the Lord's leadership, I am encouraged and discipled.

LEARN FROM THE REAL HEROES

The following people were heralded as American heroes:

- Bruce Jenner, former Olympic gold medalist, transgendered to Caitlyn Jenner—winner of the ESPN ESPY Arthur Ashe Courage Award[1]

- Jason Collins, first openly gay player in the NBA heralded by President Obama as a new role model for youth. *Washington Times*[2]

- Ellen DeGeneres, comedian and television host, has won numerous Daytime Emmy Awards and other industry awards since revealing that she is a lesbian in 1997.[3]

These are the names that are flashed in front of us in the media as those to be admired and imitated. Is it any wonder that we are watching an epidemic of decline in our nation? We could easily claim that role models and heroes are only for kids and teens, but I don't think so. All of us, no matter what our age, will be attracted to emulate what we sincerely admire.

Who are your heroes? Who do you consider the greatest role models you desire to imitate? Who do your kids or grandkids look up to and want to be like?

If we think we can trust the sports world, the entertainment industry, or corporate America to determine our generation's heroes, stars, and role models, we are our own fools. Surely we know better. But will we have the courage to break from the pack?

It is time we refuse to buy what the media has been selling us as our required taste for stars. We must veer off their scripts and rediscover the greatness that has made the church of Jesus Christ and also the nation of the United States strong and free. I think that may be what is beginning to happen as I watched the prayer film *War Room* win "the battle of the box office" upon its launch.[4]

It will take effort, and it will take focus, but I know that it can be done with God's help if we take the effort to step off the beaten path.

At the time I am writing this book a man named Dr. Ben Carson has become a household word. Perhaps by the time this book gets into your hands, you will know his name very well; or perhaps his rise to political influence has already faded. But whatever happens to him politically will never dampen his incredible life story. Carson rose out of deep poverty and school failure because of a mother who insisted he and his brother read two books a week and write reports for her on what they learned. You see, his precious mother worked for financially successful people and noticed that the people she worked for spent very little time watching television, as they were always reading books. She wanted her sons to make it out of her neighborhood, so she chose a different path for her boys. Even though, unbeknownst to them, she was unable to read herself![5] Now that is a real life hero!

We could say this message is only for those with children and grandchildren they want to shape, but I think that is a cop out. Many of us in this generation are going to be called upon to do hard things. We desperately need role models...no matter what our age. Hebrews 2, with its hall of faith listing, is a great place to renew our mind as to what a real hero looks like. Then when we finish with Hebrews 2, we should read on to Hebrews 12:1–3.

Let's compare the lukewarm believers complaining online to my grandaddy who spent his whole life defending and declaring the gospel. The difference is quite apparent. My grandad is among our great cloud of witnesses, along with the mothers of Enoch, Noah, and Moses, cheering us on today as we resist this dark flood and become the Lord's standard.

Action Steps

Here are some great ways to find the real heroes again and build our own lives of courage and faith:

1. Be willing to read books again! Dare to turn off the electronics and dig past the sound bites and Hollywood staging. Go for the biographies. And if the biographies are too long and intense, find the shorter anthologies that help you make quicker progress in your reading.

2. Enter the world of audiobooks. If you do not have the time or desire to read, keep an audio book ready on an electronic device. Many free or low-cost sites are available online, including your local public library.

3. Choose your video selections wisely. What if you intentionally looked for the hero messages instead of the special effects?

4. Develop a detective attitude toward anyone the media lifts up as a "hero" today. Ask yourself tough questions about his or her life. Does their character demonstrate the celebratory traits of the kingdom? What would Jesus say about this person's life contribution?

5. Be willing to debrief your team about the people you are holding up to honor. Inject a new idea to your team about the heroes you discover.

6. Go talk to the elder generation. Their stories of heroism trump many of our modern-day tales.

EPHESIANS 5 YOUR LIFE

If an alien from another planet wanted to gauge the moral condition of America based on the recent Emmy Awards, what conclusions would that alien draw?

—Dr. Michael Brown

That was the question Dr. Michael Brown asked in 2015 when *Game of Thrones,* the hit HBO series, was awarded the Emmy for Outstanding Drama, for this was also the same series that received a negative rating of 5 out of 5 stars for both violence and sex on the Common Sense Media website.[1] Brown goes on to say, "The saturation of sexual perversion, glorification of gender confusion, extreme violence, profanity, and substance abuse paints a terrible picture of America in 2015, making us wonder again if entertainment influences culture, reflects culture, or is a combination of both."[2]

But to intensify the picture just painted, imagine that this same alien visitor had spied on America in the early 1960s and watched some of our hit TV programming back then—shows like *The Andy Griffith Show, The Flintstones,* and *Bonanza.* Would he have believed he was visiting the same planet and country? Just imagine him reporting back to his people saying, "America has gone from *Leave It to Beaver* to *Game of Thrones*." It really boggles the mind. I agree.

These changes, however, are not limited to the entertainment industry. The F-bomb is dropped into conversation with such frequency you would think it a common grammar article. Children are using profanity at younger and younger ages. Sex is licensed for whatever fits the imagination.[3] And we are left wondering how we would ever get back to *Leave It to Beaver*!

Some would argue that we need to excuse the changing language styles toward the profane as an expression of the evolution of communication that is common with every generation. Truly even the definition of what is profane seems to have shifted. *The Wall Street Journal* attempts to explain the changes in how we judge what is "profane" and therefore off-limits in this way. "Taboos are about what we fear. In one era, it is the wrath of God; in another, hanky-panky; in ours, the defamation of groups."[4]

So I guess what they are saying is this: Prior generations feared the wrath of God. But this generation fears defaming a group of people. So that is why cursing God is okay in entertainment, but slurring a group of people will get you bleeped.

Does it matter whether we as believers give in to the cultural styles of the day and loosen up our tongue? Can we modernize our views to fit in a little easier to the current culture without risking the judgement of our God? After all, we do not want to be so out-of-step with the modern era that we lose our younger generation, all for the sake of semantics and religiosity!

Here is my answer to that question: modernize to the styles going on around us all you want, as long as you are willing to first "Ephesians 5-ize" your life!

As long as we are stacking our life up against Ephesians 5:1–21, I think we will make the right decisions. (And no, I do not believe those words of Scripture mean anything different than exactly what they say!)

Here is our dividing-line standard of Ephesians 5:1–21:

> Follow God's example, therefore, as dearly loved children and walk in the way of love, just as Christ loved us and gave himself up for us as a fragrant offering and sacrifice to God.

But among you there must not be even a hint of sexual immorality, or of any kind of impurity, or of greed, because these are improper for God's holy people. Nor should there be obscenity, foolish talk or coarse joking, which are out of place, but rather thanksgiving. For of this you can be sure: No immoral, impure or greedy person—such a person is an idolater—has any inheritance in the kingdom of Christ and of God. Let no one deceive you with empty words, for because of such things God's wrath comes on those who are disobedient. Therefore do not be partners with them.

For you were once darkness, but now you are light in the Lord. Live as children of light (for the fruit of the light consists in all goodness, righteousness and truth) and find out what pleases the Lord. Have nothing to do with the fruitless deeds of darkness, but rather expose them. It is shameful even to mention what the disobedient do in secret. But everything exposed by the light becomes visible—and everything that is illuminated becomes a light. This is why it is said:

Wake up, sleeper,
    rise from the dead,
    and Christ will shine on you.

Be very careful, then, how you live—not as unwise but as wise, making the most of every opportunity, because the days are evil. Therefore do not be foolish, but understand what the Lord's will is. Do not get drunk on wine, which leads to debauchery. Instead, be filled with the Spirit, speaking to one another with psalms, hymns, and songs from the Spirit. Sing and make music from your heart to the Lord, always giving thanks to God the Father for everything, in the name of our Lord Jesus Christ.

Action Steps

Submit to one another out of reverence for Christ. Here are some tips to make this scripture your own standard:

1. Take time to read this scripture slowly.

2. Take this scripture to the Lord and let your life stack up against what the words say. Ask Him to convict your heart in light of what this scripture reveals. Be willing to repent as necessary.

3.   Consider taking this passage of Scripture to your ark-building teammates. Study it together. Let the words become your group's standard.

4.   Do not receive this scripture apologetically with an "I'm sorry but…" attitude. Do not be ashamed of it or hide it from those whom you know need this help. Celebrate the holiness that God calls holiness! Live bold and free and happy!

5.   Learn to guard your own heart. Surrounding ourselves with those who mock this passage and live in direct opposition to its standards dulls our own spiritual sensitivity, even if we do not enter into their sin with them. Back people out of your life if necessary. Do not give up on your missionary outreach to them, but learn the art of erecting proper relationship boundaries that protect your own purity and witness.

6.   Sometimes Ephesians 5-ing your life will call for bold measures. Learn to get up and leave the movie or show when necessary. Dare to let others know when you are offended by their words. Sometimes Christians have learned to be so polite and quiet that others around us have failed to even know when there is a legitimate problem! Let your light shine lovingly and clearly without timidity and fear. Use words when necessary.

DUMP THE STRESS...
NO REALLY!

A petite Japanese cleaning consultant named Maria Kondo took the world by storm with her *The New York Times* number one bestseller *The Life-Changing Magic of Tidying Up: The Japanese Art of Decluttering and Organizing.*[1] Everywhere I went I heard people talking about her book, so last summer on vacation I checked it out. A couple of hours later, I understood the excitement. She claimed she had cracked the code to the peaceful minimalist lifestyle people secretly longed for.

Please don't think me critical. I enjoyed her ideas and have even adopted some of her principles (although we parted company when she wanted me to sit down and have a conversation with my clothes!). But what I really discovered in her book's popularity is what I already suspected. Everyone is looking for a stress-free uncluttered life.

You may be wondering what a chapter on stress is doing in this book. My answer is very simple. If we do not grab on to the Lord's grace (the beautiful flood) to reduce our stress levels, we are going to have a hard time weathering the increased pressure of the dark flood. It is that simple.

At this season in our lives as Christians, we are not able to predict how much pressure we will need to endure. However, we are foreseeing something ahead that is more difficult, not less. Because of this, we need to find ways *now* to lower our daily stress.

This is not a new thought for me as I am sure it is not new for you. The problem is how we would go about reducing the stress. I can't give back one of my kids. Or quit my job. Or stay on vacation all year long. Or not take care of my aging parents. So how am I going to reduce my stress?

Perhaps you are working on that right now as you are reading, or perhaps you have resigned yourself to always being overworked, exhausted, burned-out, and anxious. Before you throw in the towel and resign yourself to a stressed-out life, please consider this fact:

God wants you to live at peace—perfect peace. Peace that goes beyond human understanding and transcends human circumstances (Phil. 4:7). Do you believe that? Or have you become so accustomed to your stressed-out state that you cannot even imagine that I might be right?

Here is what I have discovered: stress and busyness can be addictive. We can literally get so stuck in our mild (or extreme) anxiety that we consider something to be wrong when we are not feeling stressed! I know because I have personally experienced this problem.

However, I also know this. My God can move in with His grace and release us from our worry-filled, stressed-out lives. He can restore our joy and give us back our strength. He can delight us with His powerful grace and cause us to soar on His wings like eagles above all of our troublesome problems. He can cause us to laugh at adversity and rest in His provision so that we can truly say like the great hymn writer who had just suffered the greatest anguish of his life: "It Is Well With My Soul."[2]

I am testifying to you now. I should not be able to do what I do. I have too many responsibilities and way too many stressors on my life. But here is my secret: I don't do what I do. Years ago, God gave me revelation of one single Bible verse that broke the back on my stress-o-meter: Galatians 2:20:

I have been crucified with Christ and I no longer live, but Christ lives in me. The life I now live in the body, I live by faith in the Son of God, who loved me and gave himself for me.

Here is what the Lord taught me that changed my life: I am a dead woman. I no longer live. Jesus lives His life through me. So I can rest. He carries my burdens. He solves my problems. He gives me His joy. He floods my life with His peace. Because He Himself is peace. My only job is faith.

Are you ready to lower your stress level and truly learn to trust in your Jesus? Do you want to find His joy that can never be quenched by whatever this world might throw at us? Are you willing to let Him develop a new peace in you that will challenge your current habits?

Let's go at this from one more direction. Instead of trying real hard again to "break your bad stress" habit, try *increasing* a new habit. The habit of *joy*. What if you purposed to enjoy every single moment of your life with Him. Wouldn't your stress level naturally lower as you found the joy of the Lord brings you new strength? (Neh. 8:10).

Action Steps for Stepping in to Joy and Releasing Stress

1. Decide you will not tolerate a life of stress.

2. Ask God for the breakthrough. Receive His wisdom and do what He says to do, focusing on the new change, not dwelling on the old failure.

3. Meditate on Galatians 2:20.

4. Memorize Philippians 4:4–8. Live in those verses until you engraft them into your soul.

5. Intentionally laugh every day. Several times. I cannot tell you how this began to help me!

6. Develop a habit of smiling. It actually cultivates the joy in your heart.

7.   Make your house a place of parties and joy. Look for every oppor-
     tunity to enjoy each other's company. Do not allow a week to go
     by without making intentional times of fellowship and laughter
     and fun!

8.   Help your children and teens with this. They are under increased
     pressure also!

9.   Go to frontlinefamilies.org for some resource links to help increase
     your joy.

PREPARE FOR AN EMERGENCY

Maybe you have a Christian prepper friend who has bought a six-month supply of dried food, stored enough ammo to hold off a small army, and owns every water purification device advertised on World Net Daily and Glenn Beck combined. Maybe you are envious of all their advanced planning. Or maybe you think they are crazy and are giving us all a bad name.

Whichever response is you, please know you are not alone. What to do about emergency prep is a very sticky subject. I, like you, wish I knew which response in the paragraph above will prove correct! But, alas, I do not. I am stuck like you finding my way through the myriad varieties of approaches to making the prudent preparations.

I have read all kinds of predictions of what could happen in America as a result of the dark flood. And, for all I know, by the time you read this book some of those dire predictions could have actually materialized.

Or, maybe not. Maybe life as we know it is remarkably uninterrupted in our entire lifetime. Our only hope is to lean on the Holy Spirit for wisdom. Preparing for every possible disaster is unrealistic and impossible. Global economic meltdown, power grid failure, or nuclear disaster is overwhelming even to imagine let alone prepare for.

Here are three facts that are important to consider. First, we must note that the current level of our government's wisdom and maturity is not very impressive. Hurricane Katrina taught us to not look to our government as God. Second, the nature of mankind is wicked. We have no reason to believe that a godly response would prevail should America ever face disaster. Third, God calls His people to be ready to minister salvation and comfort in the face of adversity.

Obviously, our most important preparations must be spiritual. God has a remarkable way of preserving and leading His children in times of famine and corruption. Check out the Old Testament for examples such as manna in the wilderness (Exod. 16) and Joseph storing grain (Gen. 41).

What natural preparations do you feel the Lord is leading you to make? Whatever they are, just do them. Obey His leading in a timely way.

Below are some of the things we have prepared for our home. We live within a few miles of the great New Madrid fault, so our preparations are also important should the long predicted earthquake ever come. If you go to the FEMA website as a starting point, you can learn the basics of what our own government advises.

Emergency Preparation Supplies We Have Addressed

1. Portable water purification system and extra bottled water
2. Extra emergency food (Enough for a few weeks...not months)
3. Three-day emergency supply buckets for each person per the guidelines on the FEMA website
4. Cook stove and extra fuel
5. Flashlights and extra batteries
6. Firewood (which can be our heat source)
7. First aid supplies

Other supplies might include generators, gasoline, and other energy sources. Having cash and/or precious metals available is, of course, important also.

We have talked as a family and worked on some guidelines and instructions for our children. We have found it important to help our children face these uncertain times with both confidence and faith. Should the Lord lead us to make other preparations over time, we have purposed to obey in confidence. So now we rest in faith.

What do you and your family need to do to follow the Lord's lead and walk in peace? Follow His directions, not mine!

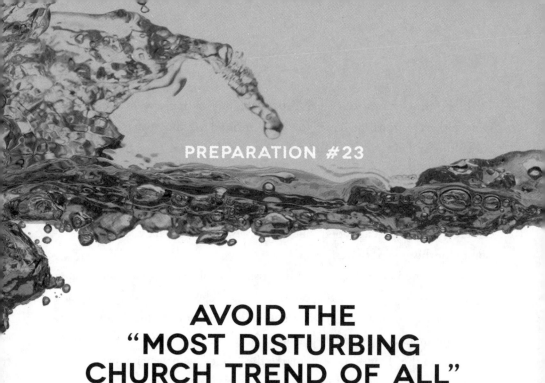

AVOID THE
"MOST DISTURBING
CHURCH TREND OF ALL"

This article title lured me in: "The Most Disturbing Church Trend of All."[1] I figured it would outline yet another dark trend of heresy that I needed to pray against. So I was rather shocked when I read the author's conclusion: "Specifically, in the last two years, I have seen one common thread become a common rope. I have never seen a problem discussed this commonly amid a diversity of church sizes and denominational affiliations."

What is this one problem? It's that your most committed people will attend worship services less frequently than ever in 2015.

What does this mean? Simply that people who used to attend four times a month may only attend three times a month. Members who used to come twice a month will only come once a month."[2]

Obviously, what is being identified here is *not* the phenomenon of people falling away altogether, but instead the problem of sagging stability and reduced commitment. So why are we attending church less frequently?

Three factors have been identified, including an increase in competitive sport and recreational activities for kids on Sundays, the greater mobility of our culture and virtual workplace arrangements that cause more travel, and the access to online church services so people can stay home and yet go to church in their living room.[3]

The effect on church strength has been significant…and this problem we cannot blame on the dark flood "out there." We are going to have to take responsibility for this one ourselves.

Last year the internet was abuzz discussing sociologists Packard and Hope's book, *Church Refugees*.[4] In this book they researched the trend of previously active and vibrant members of churches who drop out of church attendance while still maintaining their personal faith commitments. The researches named them the "Dones" (as opposed to the "nones" who were named by other researchers as those who did not name any faith commitment.) They appear to be done with "church" but not done with Jesus. Probably many of us who are reading this book know people in that category.

This leads me to some sticky questions.

Is this shift in commitment to the local church going to serve us well in the midst of what is going on in our nation right now? Are these patterns, in fact, dangerous, and will they further weaken our collective ability to weather the dark flood around us? What would happen if all of us followed these trends?

(I am speaking strongly here, so be warned.)

You probably already know what I will be proposing here, but let me just state the obvious: We cannot and should not give up on local churches in America. We really do need each other!

Hebrews 10:24–26 is very clear:

> And let us consider how we may spur one another on toward love and good deeds. Let us not give up meeting together, as some are in the habit doing, but let us encourage one another—and all the more as you see the Day approaching.

Forsaking the assembling of the brethren is not a good idea at any time, but is especially dangerous when we need to be praying together in agreement, preaching the gospel for salvation, discipling young believers, and helping to debrief our teammates! Maybe the church is in need of an overhaul in America, but dropping out and becoming lone rangers is not the answer.

Action Steps

Here is what we can do to avoid the most dangerous trend:

1. Repent.

2. We need to examine our priorities to the Lord and to our fellow brothers and sisters in Christ. We may need to tell the kids no when it comes to Sunday morning sports. We may need to sacrifice to get to church!

3. Let the Lord break our heart for Him and His people once again. Pray for the churches in America.

4. Get over "it." (See Chapter 11.) Offenses, hurts, and upsets can be healed in Jesus.

5. Be part of the solution instead of the problem. Speak words of encouragement over your local church and its leaders. Roll up your sleeves and become one of the 20 percent of the people who do 80 percent of the work.[5] Remember, we are not laboring for men but for the Lord anyway so we can work cheerfully!

TRAIN LIKE AN OLYMPIAN

Running ten miles at a time is not a big deal for some of my kids. But I am not like my kids. Running to the mailbox or using my elliptical for twenty minutes is a big deal for me. At my house, mom doesn't do things like progression regression runs or mile repeats with intervals or speed trainings. I don't set my alarm to get up at 5:00 a.m. so I can hit my first six mile run of the day and then eat my dinner early so I can digest my food before my second six mile run at bedtime. Why? Because I am not that crazy. And even more specifically, I am not in training for collegiate level running.

While workouts are definitely not my thing, I have appreciated the opportunity to watch the immense amount of effort that goes into serious athletic training. In my younger years I might have thought athletics was all about talent. But as I have watched behind the scenes, I have come to realize it is about a whole lot more.

Sacrifice. Self-discipline. Dedication. Pain. Emotional fortitude and grit. These are the characteristics that cause someone to become a champion. Champions are not born. They are developed in the ups and downs of wins and losses, successes and setbacks, excitements and disappointments.

When my husband called me into our bedroom one day several years ago and said, "Honey, I believe the Lord is calling me to train spiritually like an Olympic athlete." I, in one instant, knew what he meant. I sensed the Lord calling me to the same commitment.

What would happen in America right now if we, as God's people, began training spiritually with the same vigor and sacrifice as the most dedicated athletes among us? I believe we would see some changes in our midst. Our true question becomes this: With what we are up against in this generation. Why would we not be training ourselves spiritually as if we were in a serious race? Couch-potato Christians may not fare well in the new post-Christian America. It is time to seriously look at this issue before it is too late.

We know a man who travels to our city every couple of years to raise money for churches in some of the poorest parts of India. He is an indigenous missionary from India with a passion to both care for the children in his orphanages and also to raise support for the pastors of his area. When Doug and I are around this man, we are always convicted. His humility is unwavering. His prayers are uncannily sincere. His knowledge of the Word of God is shocking.

From the time I first met Arun, I knew there was something precious about him. It is not hard for him to draw an audience because his presence radiates the glory of God. One Sunday, we brought Arun to our family's home after church. It was Sunday dinner time, and our table was loaded with food. Since he was the honored guest, we invited Arun to take the lead in the buffet line. But in a polite way he declined our invitation. He urged others to take his place while he quietly visited with the people gathered in the living room.

Later, as a good host, I tried to get Arun back to the buffet line. That's when he said something that would forever stick in my mind. "Thank you so much sister. It looks like a lovely display of food. But since I have been in the United States, I have been eating far too much. I think I must decline," he said sweetly with a tip of his head.

I stood there with my empty plate that I had intended to refill. It was a holy moment. Something was indeed different about my brother Arun. The presence and power of God that exuded from his life were not displays to impress the

Americans. They were real. And they were born at the cost of a man who had paid the price to train for spiritual reigning.

Do I think that spiritual disciplines like fasting and prayer and Bible reading will earn salvation or extra love from God? Of course not. But neither do I think the apostle Paul would have written a large portion of the New Testament if he had not been willing to live a life of sacrifice and discipline for the sake of the Kingdom. He explained it like this:

> Do you not know that in a race all the runners run, but only one gets the prize? Run in such a way as to get the prize. Everyone who competes in the games goes into strict training. They do it to get a crown that will not last, but we do it to get a crown that will last forever. Therefore I do not run like someone running aimlessly; I do not fight like a boxer beating the air. No, I strike a blow to my body and make it my slave so that after I have preached to others, I myself will not be disqualified for the prize.
>
> —1 Corinthians 9:24–27

How badly do we want to be effective? Are we willing to "train like an Olympian" that others might come to know Him? His name might be glorified and His Kingdom might be advanced in the earth!

Action Steps for Growing in Spiritual Disciplines

Desire growth in your spirit man with more passion than any other desire or hobby. Repent of laziness or indifference. Turn off the electronics and take the first steps!

1.   Recognize that a good healthy training regimen for you might look different than your friend's plan. Let God lead you to a wise balanced plan that incorporates the various disciplines recognized over the ages of the church to be central in healthy spiritual growth:

     • Prayer
     • Bible reading

- Scripture memorization
- Scripture meditation
- Worship
- Fasting
- Fellowship with believers
- Evangelism

2. Read about great men and women of God's personal lives and how they managed their time, effort, and priorities.

3. Find other believers you know who excel at various spiritual disciplines. Ask them what they know. Have them pray for you and help you grow.

4. Schedule your daily routines under the leadership of the Holy Spirit. Recognize that the little things done consistently over time often bring the biggest results. Pick one area to grow in at a time and celebrate all good results. Just like physical conditioning is improved by training incrementally, our faith is grown by increasing spiritual disciplines incrementally.

LISA'S LAST WORD

This seems like a fitting chapter to end our time together. I believe God is raising up a generation who is serious about their faith and is passionate to resist the dark flood as they throw themselves headlong into the beautiful presence of our savior.

I have been so blessed with the opportunity to write this book. If no one ever read it, it would truly have been worth it in my life and my family's and friends' lives. I am a changed woman. Filled with hope, I am excited to face our future days together with joy and trust in our King.

This is our hour.

You are my brothers and sisters.

I stand with you shoulder to shoulder in the most glorious privilege ever imaginable.

To bring glory to our King.

I will be praying for you and continuing to write to you.

Will you do the same for me?

—Blessings,
Lisa

NOTES

Introduction

1. Russell Goldman, "Here's a List of 58 Gender Options for Facebook Users," ABCNews.com, published February 13, 2014, accessed October 21, 2015, http://abcnews.go.com/blogs/headlines/2014/02/heres-a-list-of-58-gender-options-for-facebook-users/.

2. Dana Olwan and Sophia Azeb, "Reframing the Discussion: Concluding Thoughts on the Forum on Muslim Feminisms," TheFeministWire.com, published August 5, 2012, accessed October 21, 2015, http://www.thefeministwire.com/2012/08/reframing-the-discussion-concluding-thoughts-on-the-forum-on-muslim-feminisms/.

3. Brittany M. Hughes, "Abortion Supporter Tells Congress That Dismembering a LIVE Fetus Is 'Humane'," MRCTV.org, published September 9, 2015, accessed October 21, 2015, http://www.mrctv.org/blog/abortion-supporter-tells-congress-dismembering-fetus-humane#.focnn7:S8Di. Edited clip with transcript of Planned Parenthood before Congress: "I believe, for a fetus, for a pre-viable fetus, yes. A D&E (dismemberment of a fetus) procedure is a very humane procedure and it protects the woman and her health and safety more than any other procedure." —Priscilla Smith, a director and senior fellow at the Program for the Study of Reproductive Justice at Yale Law School, Unedited version: http://www.c-span.org/video/?328011-1/hearing-planned-parenthood.

4. Valerie Richardson, "Houston transgender bathroom bill debate centers on differing definitions of 'men'," published October 5, 2015, accessed October 21, 2015, http://www.washingtontimes.com/news/2015/oct/5/houston-transgender-bathroom-bill-debate-centers-o/.

5. Matthew Vines, MatthewVines.com.

6. "Attorney: Kim Davis Had to Change Phone Number Because of Death Threats," The O'Reilly Factor, published September 14, 2015, accessed October 21, 2015, http://insider .foxnews.com/2015/09/14/attorney-mat-staver-kim-davis-receiving-death-threats-had-change -phone-number. Kyle Mantyla, "Mat Staver Claims *The View* called for Kim Davis to be killed [Updated]," published September 16, 2015, accessed October 21, 2015, http://www.right wingwatch.org/content/mat-staver-claims-view-called-kim-davis-be-killed. Matt Barber, "Burn Kim Davis Alive!," CharismaNews.com, published September 14, 2015, accessed October 21, 2015, http://www.charismanews.com/opinion/clarion-call/51971-burn-kim-davis-alive.

7. Occupy Wall Street, accessed October 22, 2015, http://occupywallst.org/about/.

Chapter 1
The Deluge of the Dark Flood

1. Eric Metaxas, *Bonhoeffer: Pastor, Martyr, Prophet, Spy* (Thomas Nelson, 2011).

2. "*Obergefell ET AL. v. Hodge*s, Director, Ohio Department of Health, ET AL.", *Supreme Court of the United States*, October Term 2014, accessed October 21, 2015, http://www.supremecourt .gov/opinions/14pdf/14-556_3204.pdf.

3. Ibid.

4. Ibid.

5. Ibid.

6. All headlines from Charisma News: charismanews.com.

7. John S. Dickson, *The Great Evangelical Recession* (Baker Books, 2013), 41.

8. Dickson, *The Great Evangelical Recession*, 41.

9. Edwin W. Lutzer, *Where Do We Go From Here? Hope and Direction in Our Present Crisis* (Moody Publishers, 2013), 5.

10. "Synod president responds to SCOTUS same-sex marriage ruling," *The Lutheran Church Missouri Synod News and Information*, published June 26, 2015, accessed October 22, 2015, http://blogs.lcms.org/2015/synod-president-responds-to-scotus-same-sex-marriage-ruling.

11. Craig Schneider, "Southern Baptist Convention's statement opposing same-sex marriage," AJC.com, published June 17, 2015, accessed October 22, 2015, http://www.ajc.com/news /news/local/southern-baptists-statement-opposing-gay-marriage/nmfLH/.

12. George O. Wood, "Statement Regarding the Supreme Court's Same-Sex Marriage Decision," PENews.org, published June 26, 2015, accessed October 22, 2015, http://penews .org/Article/Statement-Regarding-the-Supreme-Court-s-Same-Sex-Marriage-Decision/.

13. Franklin Graham, "God Hears the Prayers of His People, and Walls Can Be Rebuilt," *Billy Graham Evangelistic Association*, published August 31, 2015, accessed October 22, 2015, http:// billygraham.org/story/franklin-graham-god-hears-the-prayers-of-his-people-and-walls-can-be -rebuilt/.

Chapter 2
We Are Still Not Ready

1. Larry Norman, "I Wish We'd All Been Ready," SongLyrics.com, accessed October 22, 2015, http://www.songlyrics.com/larry-norman/i-wish-we-d-all-been-ready-lyrics/.

2. Hal Lindsey, *The Late Great Planet Earth* (Zondervan, 1970).

Chapter 3
The Rules Changed in Post-Christian America

1. William J. Federer, *America's God and Country: Encyclopedia of Quotations* (Amerisearch, 2000), 695.

2. Kristy Etheridge/BGEA, "UK Prime Minister Just Said What President Obama Should Be Saying," CharismaNews.com, published April 8, 2015, accessed October 22, 2015, http://www.charismanews.com/world/49096-uk-prime-minister-just-said-what-president-obama-should-be-saying.

3. "America's Changing Religious Landscape," *Pew Research Center*, published May 12, 2015, accessed October 22, 2015, http://www.pewforum.org/2015/05/12/americas-changing-religious-landscape/.

4. Of or relating to the religious writings, beliefs, values, or traditions held in common by Judaism (the Old Testament) and Christianity (the New Testament). Note: Information in parentheses added by author to bring clarity. "Judeo-Christian," Dictionary.com, accessed October 22, 2015, http://dictionary.reference.com/browse/judeo-christian.

5. http://www.peggynoonan.com/47/. Ravi Zacharias, *Deliver Us From Evil* (Thomas Nelson, 1998).

6. Saul D. Alinsky, *Rules for Radicals: A Practical Primer for Realistic Radicals* (Vintage, 1989).

7. "Essay: Radical Saul Alinsky: Prophet of Power to the People," *Time* magazine, March 2, 1970, accessed October 22, 2015, http://content.time.com/time/subscriber/article/0,33009,904228-1,00.html.

8. "Playboy Interview: Saul Alinsky," *Playboy* magazine, March 1972. Author's note: This 1972 article is frequently referenced. I read portions of the interview in various articles. I chose not to view the original *Playboy* article myself. "Empowering People, Not Elites," Progress.org, published December 31, 2003, accessed October 22, 2015, http://www.progress.org/archive/empowering-people-not-elites.

9. Alinsky, *Rules for Radicals*, 3.

10. Stanley Kurtz, "Why Hillary's Alinsky Letters Matter," *National Review*, September 22, 2014, accessed October 22, 2015, http://www.nationalreview.com/corner/388560/why-hillarys-alinsky-letters-matter-stanley-kurtz.

11. Cameron Van de Graaf, "*The 'Big Lie' Exposed: A Rhetorical Analysis of Nazi-German in 22 Lessons*," Hoover Institution, published December 17, 2014, accessed October 22, 2015, http://www.hoover.org/news/big-lie-exposed-rhetorical-analysis-nazi-german-22-lessons.

12. Alinsky, *Rules for Radicals*.

13. Steven Ertelt, "10th Video Catches Planned Parenthood: We Sell 'Fresh' Aborted Baby Eyes, Hearts and 'Gonads'," LifeNews.com, published September 15, 2015, accessed October 22, 2015, http://www.lifenews.com/2015/09/15/10th-video-catches-planned-parenthood-we-sell -fresh-aborted-baby-eyes-hearts-and-gonads/. "Planned Parenthood Practices," C-SPAN, September 9, 2015, accessed October 22, 2015, http://www.c-span.org/video/?328011-1 /hearing-planned-parenthood.

14. Katy Osborn, "How ESPN Decided to Give Courage Award to Caitlyn Jenner," *Time* magazine, published July 13, 2015, accessed October 22, 2015, http://time.com/3955433 /caitlyn-jenner-espy-award/.

15. Office of the Press Secretary, "Executive Order—Using Behavioral Science Insights to Better Serve the American People," *The White House*, published September 15, 2015, accessed October 22, 2105, https://www.whitehouse.gov/the-press-office/2015/09/15/executive-order-using -behavioral-science-insights-better-serve-american.

16. Donald Marron, "Obama's Nudge Brigade: White House Embraces Behavioral Sciences To Improve Government," *Forbes*, published September 16, 2015, accessed October 22, 2015, http://www.forbes.com/sites/beltway/2015/09/16/obama-nudge-government/.

17. Richard H. Thaler, *Nudge: Improving Decisions About Health, Wealth, and Happiness* (Penguin Books, Revised and Expanded Edition 2009).

18. "Declaration of Independence," Archives.gov, accessed October 22, 2015, http://www .archives.gov/exhibits/charters/declaration_transcript.html.

19. "What Does the Religion of Peace Teach About…Lying (Taqiyya and Kitman)," TheReligionofPeace.com, accessed October 22, 2015, http://www.thereligionofpeace.com /quran/011-taqiyya.htm.

20. "Washington's 'Earnest Prayer'," USHistory.org, accessed October 22, 2015, http://www .ushistory.org/valleyforge/washington/earnestprayer.html.

21. Example: "Baptism of Pocahontas," Architect of the Capitol, accessed October 22, 2015, aoc.gov/capitol-hill/historic-rotunda-paintings/baptism-pocahontas.

22. Samuel James Smith, "The New-England Primer," *Encyclopaedia Britannica*, accessed October 22, 2015, http://www.britannica.com/topic/The-New-England-Primer.

23. "Religion," *Gallup*, accessed October 22, 2015, http://www.gallup.com/poll/1690/religion .aspx.

24. Stoyan Zaimov, "Is America a Christian Nation? New Poll Suggests Few Americans View the US as a Christian Country," ChristianPost.com, published July 31, 2015, accessed October 22, 2015, http://www.christianpost.com/news/is-america-a-christian-nation-new-poll-suggests -few-americans-view-the-us-as-a-christian-country-142124/.

25. "Obama's 2006 Speech on Faith and Politics," *The New York Times*, published June 28, 2006, accessed October 22, 2015, http://www.nytimes.com/2006/06/28/us/politics /2006obamaspeech.html?pagewanted=all&_r=0.

Chapter 4
Exiled in Our Own Nation

1. Rod Dreher, "Orthodox Christians Must Now Learn to Live as Exiles in Our Own Country," *Time* magazine, published June 26, 2015, accessed October 22, 2015, http://time.com /3938050/orthodox-christians-must-now-learn-to-live-as-exiles-in-our-own-country/.

2. Russell Moore, "Is America Post-Christian?," RussellMoore.com, published May 26, 2015, accessed October 22, 2015, https://www.russellmoore.com/2015/05/26/is-america-post -christian/.

3. Dreher, "Orthodox Christians Must Now Learn to Live as Exiles in Our Own Country," *Time* magazine, June 26, 2015.

4. Elisabeth Kübler-Ross, *On Death and Dying: What the Dying Have to Teach Doctors, Nurses, Clergy and Their Own Families* (Scribner, Reprint Edition, 2014).

Chapter 5
When the Flood Hits Our Front Door

1. Warren Richey, "Poll finds broad, rapid shift among Americans toward gay marriage," *The Christian Science Monitor*, March 27, 2014, accessed October 22, 2014, http://www.csmonitor .com/USA/Politics/2014/0327/Poll-finds-broad-rapid-shift-among-Americans-toward-gay -marriage.

2. Michael L. Brown, *Can You Be Gay and Christian?: Responding With Love and Truth to Questions About Homosexuality* (Lake Mary, FL: Frontline, 2014), 1.

Chapter 6
Why *Coexist* Will Not Work

1. "Coexistence," Coexistence.Art.Museum.com, accessed October 22, 2015, http://www .coexistence.art.museum/Coex/Index.asp.

2. Raphie Etgar, "Museum on the Seam Statement: Image of Coexistence Traveling the World," @U2, published July 11, 2005, accessed October 22, 2015, http://www.atu2.com/news/museum -on-the-seam-statement-image-of-coexistence-traveling-the-world.html. Sean Curnyn, "Bono in 'Son of God' Shocker," *The Cinch Review*, published June 25, 2013, accessed October 22, 2015, http://www.cinchreview.com/bono-in-son-of-god-shocker/10496/.

3. Ted Ryan, "The Making of 'I'd Like to Buy the World a Coke'," *Coca-Cola Journey*, published January 1, 2012, accessed October 22, 2105, http://www.coca-colacompany.com/stories/coke -lore-hilltop-story/.

4. "It's a Small World," Walt Disney World, accessed October 22, 2015, https://disneyworld .disney.go.com/attractions/magic-kingdom/its-a-small-world/.

5. "The History of 'VISUALIZE WORLD PEACE'," PeaceVision.org, accessed October 22, 2015, http://peacevision.org/origins.html.

6. Thomas More, *Utopia* (Penguin Classics Reissue Edition, 2003).

7. "Ever After: A Cinderella Story," imdb.com, accessed October 22, 2015, http://www.imdb.com/title/tt0120631/.

8. "Utopia, Sir Thomas More: General Summary," SparkNotes.com, accessed October 22, 2015, http://www.sparknotes.com/philosophy/utopia/summary.html.

9. Linda K. Salvucci, "We Need a STEM-Like Initative for History," HistoryNewsNetwork.org, published June 19, 2011, accessed October 22, 2015, http://historynewsnetwork.org/article/140054.

10. *Global Citizen,* accessed October 22, 2015, https://www.globalcitizen.org/en/.

11. "Transforming our world: the 2030 Agenda for Sustainable Development," United Nations Sustainable Development Knowledge Platform, published September 27, 2015, accessed October 22, 2015, https://sustainabledevelopment.un.org/post2015/transformingourworld.

12. Michelle Boorstein, "In a first, Washington National Cathedral to host Friday Muslim prayer service," *The Washington Post*, published November 10, 2014, accessed October 22, 2015, https://www.washingtonpost.com/local/in-a-first-washington-national-cathedral-to-host-regular-friday-muslim-prayer/2014/11/10/53d3425e-6916-11e4-9fb4-a622dae742a2_story.html.

13. Stoyan Zaimov, "World's First Openly Lesbian Bishop to Remove Crosses, Build Islamic Prayer Room in Swedish Seamen's Church," *The Christian Post*, published October 7, 2015, accessed October 22, 2015, http://www.christianpost.com/news/worlds-first-openly-lesbian-bishop-to-remove-crosses-build-islamic-prayer-room-in-swedish-seamens-church-147095/.

14. Cynthia Littleton/REUTERS, "How Prayer Helped Oprah Out of a Dark Place," Charisma News, published October 16, 2015, accessed October 22, 2015, http://www.charismanews.com/culture/52672-how-prayer-helped-oprah-out-of-a-dark-place.

15. "Interview of the President by Al Arabiya," The White House, October 4, 2007, accessed October 22, 2015, http://georgewbush-whitehouse.archives.gov/news/releases/2007/10/2007 1005-5.html.

16. Stephen Prothero, *God Is Not One: The Eight Rival Religions That Run the World* (HarperOne Reprint Edition, 2011), 3.

Chapter 7
The Powerful, Beautiful Flood I Did Not Know

1. Stephen Reed Cattley, ed., *The Acts and Monuments of John Foxe: A New and Complete Edition, Volume 3* (London: R. B. Seeley & W. Burnside, 1837), accessed online October 21, 2015, https://goo.gl/dND1gV.

2. "Frances Jane van Alystyne (Fanny Crosby) 1820–1915, Hymn Writer," European American Evangelistic Crusades, accessed October 21, 2015, http://www.eaec.org/faithhallfame/fanny_crosby.htm.

3. Eric Metaxas, *Bonhoeffer: Pastor, Martyr, Prophet, Spy* (Thomas Nelson, 2011), 531.

4. Ibid., 532.

5. Brother Lawrence, *The Practice of the Presence of God* (Whitaker House, 1982).

6. Martin Luther, "A Mighty Fortress Is Our God," 1529, Public Domain.

7. John Wesley, *Journal of John Wesley*, accessed October 21, 2015, http://www.ccel.org/ccel/wesley/journal.vi.ii.xvi.html.

8. Andrew Murray, *Abide in Christ*, (Whitaker House, 2002).

9. Elisabeth Elliot, *Secure in the Everlasting Arms* (Grand Rapids, MI: Revell, 2004).

10. "We Will Sing Live - Brother of two Christian victims of ISIS calls in," SAT7 Network, published on Feb 18, 2015, accessed October 21, 2015, https://www.youtube.com/watch?v=hIEqjMm7BOg.

Chapter 8
How to Step In to the Flood

1. John Burton, *The Coming Church* (Significant Publishing, Revised 2014), 156.

2. Christian Chiakulas, "Churches Could Fill Their Pews With Millennials If They Just Did This," *Huffington Post*, published September 30, 2015, accessed October 22, 2015, http://www.huffingtonpost.com/christian-chiakulas/churches-millennials-if-they-just-did-this_b_8215846.html.

3. Dietrich Bonhoeffer, *The Cost of Discipleship* (New York, NY: Touchstone, 1995).

Chapter 9
The Standard

1. John Gill, *John Gill's Exposition of the Entire Bible* (BibleStudyTools.com), accessed October 21, 2015, http://www.biblestudytools.com/commentaries/gills-exposition-of-the-bible/isaiah-59-19.html.

2. "5251-NES," *Strong's Concordance*, accessed October 22, 2015, biblehub.com/hebrew/5251.htm.

3. "I'm Christian, But I'm Not," *BuzzFeedYellow*, published September 7, 2015, accessed October 21, 2015, https://www.youtube.com/watch?v=5bWHSpmXEJs&feature=yout.be.

Chapter 10
The Promise That Will Never Fail

1. Chelsen Vicari, *Distortion: How the New Christian Left Is Twisting the Gospel and Damaging the Faith* (Lake Mary, FL: Frontline, 2014), xiii.

2. Will Graham, "The Tree Stump Prayer: When Billy Graham Overcame Doubt," *Billy Graham Evangelistic Association*, July 9, 2014, accessed October 22, 2015, http://billygraham.org/story/the-tree-stump-prayer-where-billy-graham-overcame-doubt/.

Chapter 11
The Ark We Are Permitted to Build

1. Lily Rothman, "Remember Y2K? Here's How We Prepped for the Non-Disaster," *Time* magazine, December 31, 2014, accessed October 22, 2015, http://time.com/3645828/y2k-look-back/.

2. Alec Hogg, "As inequality soars, the nervous super rich are already planning their escapes," *The Guardian*, January 23, 2015, accessed October 22, 2015, http://theguardian.com/public-leaders-network/2015/jan/23/nervous-super-rich-planning-escapes-davos-2015.

3. Dreher, "Orthodox-christians-must-now-learn-to-live-as-exiles-in-our-own-country."

4. Ibid.

5. Rod Dreher, "Critics of the Benedict Option," *The American Conservative*, July 8, 2015, accessed October 22, 2015, http://www.theamericanconservative.com/dreher/critics-of-the-benedict-option/. John Zmirak, "The Benedict Option Isn't One," *Intercollegiate Review*, July 20, 2015, accessed October 22, 2015, http://www.intercollegiatereview.com/index.php/2015/07/20/the-benedict-option-isnt-one/.

Chapter 12
What Do We Do Now?

1. Andrew Murray, *Abide in Christ* (New Kensington, PA: Whitaker House, 2002).

Preparation #1
Run to the Arms of My Father

1. Dennis Jernigan, "I Will Run to the Arms of My Father," published April 1, 2012, dennisjernigan.com, accessed October 15, 2015.

Preparation #2
Check for the Elijah Errors

1. David Wilkerson, "Seven Thousand Did Not Bow," spoken April 23, 2001. WorldChallenge.org, accessed October 15, 2015, http://sermons.worldchallenge.org/en/node/1185.

2. Ibid.

Preparation #3
Come Out of the Cave

1. David Wilkerson, "Seven Thousand Did Not Bow," spoken April 23, 2001. WorldChallenge.org, accessed October 15, 2015, http://sermons.worldchallenge.org/en/node/1185.

Preparation #7
Redefine Persecution in Our Generation

1. J. Paul Nyquist and David Jeremiah (Foreword), *Prepare: Living Your Faith in an Increasingly Hostile Culture* (Chicago, IL: Moody Publishers, 2015), Introduction.

2. Sarah Eekhoff Zylstra, "'Not Forgotten': The Top 50 Countries Where It's Most Difficult To Be A Christian," ChristianityToday.com, posted 1/7/2015, accessed October 15, 2015, http:// www.christianitytoday.com/gleanings/2015/january/not-forgotten-top-50-countries-world -watch-list-open-doors.html.

3. Liberty Counsel, "'True Colors' Revealed in Kim Davis Case," CharismaNews.com, October 14, 2015, accessed October 15, 2015, http://www.charismanews.com/us/52626-true-colors -revealed-in-kim-davis-case.

4. Todd Starnes, "Football coach says he will defy school's prayer ban," FoxNews.com, October 14, 2015, accessed October 15, 2015, http://www.foxnews.com/opinion/2015/10/14/exclusive -football-coach-says-will-defy-schools-prayer-ban.html.

5. Todd Starnes, "Navy Chaplain Censored: 'Don't Pray in the Name of Jesus,'" FoxNews.com, April 22, 2015, accessed October 15, 2015, http://www.foxnews.com/opinion/2015/04/22 /navy-chaplain-censored-dont-pray-in-name-jesus.html.

6. Rick Ungar, "Ted Cruz And The False Narrative Of Christian Persecution," Forbes.com, June 10, 2015, accessed October 15, 2015, http://www.forbes.com/sites/rickungar/2015/06/10/ted -cruz-and-the-false-narrative-of-christian-persecution/.

7. Jimmy Draper, "CALL TO PRAYER: Persecution from a Chinese Christian's perspective," *Baptist Press*, May 30, 2014, accessed October 15, 2015, http://www.bpnews.net/42677/call -to-prayer-persecution-from-a-chinese-christians-perspective.

8. Heather Sells, "Gay Marriage Ruling Fallout: Christian Leaders React," CBNNews, June 27, 2015, accessed October 15, 2015, http://www1.cbn.com/cbnnews/us/2015/June/Christian -Leaders-React-to-Gay-Marriag-Ruling/.

Preparation #8
Hold On to Sound Doctrine

1. Barna, *Futurecast,* 137.

2. Christopher Yuan, "Why 'God and the Gay Christian' Is Wrong About the Bible and Same-Sex Relationships," *Christianity Today*, June 9, 2014, accessed October 17, 2015, http:// www.christianitytoday.com/ct/2014/june-web-only/why-matthew-vines-is-wrong-about-bible -same-sex-relationshi.html#bmb=1.

3. Ibid.

4. Edward W. A. Koehler, *A Summary of Christian Doctrine* (St. Louis: Concordia Publishing House, 2006), 324.

5. Thom S. Rainer, "Six Ways Millennials Are Educating Their Churches Theologically," ThomRainer.com, April 15, 2015, accessed October 17, 2015, http://thomrainer.com/2015/04 /six-ways-millennials-are-educating-their-churches-theologically/.

6. George Barna, *Futurecast: What Today's Trends Mean for Tomorrow's World* (Austin, TX: BarnaBooks, an Imprint of Tyndale House Publishers Inc., 2011), 138.

7. Koehler, *A Summary of Christian Doctrine*, 324.

8. Steve Hill, *Spiritual Avalanche: The Threat of False Teachings That Could Destroy Millions* (Lake Mary, FL: Charisma House, 2013).

9. Barna, *Futurecast*, 137.

Preparation #9
Recognize the True Church From the Apostate

1. Steve Turner, "Creed," *Up to Date* (Oxford: Lion Publishing and Hodder and Stoughton Ltd, 1982).

2. The Clergy Project, accessed October 16, 2015, http://clergyproject.org/.

3. "646. apostasia," *Strong's Concordance,* http://biblehub.com/greek/646.htm.

4. Noah Webster, "Discernment," *American Dictionary of the English Language (1828)*, accessed online October 16, 2015, http://webstersdictionary1828.com/Dictionary/discernment.

5. Daniel C. Dennett and Linda LaScola, "Preachers Who Are Not Believers," *Evolutionary Psychology*, ISSN 1474-7049—Volume 8 (1). 2010, accessed October 16, 2015, https://ase.tufts .edu/cogstud/dennett/papers/Pr deachers_who_are_not_believers.pdf.

6 Pew Forum, "America's Changing Religious Landscape," May 12, 2015, accessed October 16, 2015, http://www.pewforum.org/2015/05/12/americas-changing-religious-landscape/.

7. Ibid.

8. Mark A. Noll, "Martin Luther and the Concept of a 'True' Church," *Evangelical Quarterly*, pp. 79–85, Biblicalstudies.org, accessed October 16, 2015, http://biblicalstudies.org.uk/pdf/eq /18-2_079.pdf.

9. "Worldview Chart," Summit Ministries, summit.org, accessed October 16, 2015, https:// www.summit.org/resources/worldview-chart/.

Preparation #10
Practice Discernment Online

1. http://av1611.com/kjbp/kjv-dictionary/discern.html

2. *Strongs Greek Lexicon*, item 1253, diakrisis, accessed October 16, 2015, http://www.eliyah .com/cgi-bin/strongs.cgi?file=greeklexicon&isindex=diakrisis.

3. "Discern, Discerner, Discernment [B-1, Noun, G1253, diakrisis]", *Vine's Expository Dictionary of New Testament Words*, accessed October 16, 2015, http://studybible.info/vines /Discern,%20Discerner,%20Discernment.

4. Jeff Walton, "Rachel Held Evans Departs Evangelicalism: Are Millennials Next?," Charisma News.com, March 17, 2015, accessed October 16, 2015, http://www.charismanews.com/us /48769-rachel-held-evans-departs-evangelicalism-are-millennials-next.

5. Jennifer Golbeck, "Internet Trolls Are Narcissists, Psychopaths and Sadists," *Psychology Today*, posted September 18, 2014, accessed October 16, 2015, https://www.psychologytoday.com/blog /your-online-secrets/201409/internet-trolls-are-narcissists-psychopaths-and-sadists.

6. "Troll," Netlingo.com, accessed October 16, 2015, http://www.netlingo.com/word/troll.php.

Preparation #12
Hold On to America

1. Ronald Reagan, "Address Before a Joint Session of the Congress on the State of the Union," January 25, 1984, accessed October 18, 2015, http://www.presidency.ucsb.edu/ws/?pid=40205.

2. "Millennial Faith Participation and Retention," *Focus on the Family Findings*, published August 2013, accessed October 22, 2015, http://www.focusonthefamily.com/about_us/focus -findings/religion-and-culture/~/media/images/about-us/focus-findings/FF%20-%20 Millennial%20Faith%20Retention%20FINAL.ashx.

3. Jerry Newcombe, "An Appeal to Christians Who Do Not Plan to Vote in November," *The Christian Post*, October 29, 2014, accessed October 18, 2015, http://www.christianpost.com /news/an-appeal-to-christians-who-do-not-plan-to-vote-in-november-128826/.

4. Jeff Poor, "Cheney: 'Obama Does Not Hold the View That America Is the Exceptional Nation'," Breitbart.com, published September 1, 2015, accessed October 22, 2015, http://www .breitbart.com/video/2015/09/01/cheney-obama-does-not-hold-the-view-that-america-is-the -exceptional-nation/.

5. Todd Starnes, "School Cancels 'America Day,'" Fox News, published October 5, 2015, accessed October 22, 2015, http://www.foxnews.com/opinion/2015/10/05/school-cancels -america-day.html.

6. Michael Schaub, "Literature of 9/11 college class accused of being 'sympathetic towards terrorism'," *Los Angeles Times*, published September 1, 2015, accessed October 22, 2015, http:// www.latimes.com/books/jacketcopy/la-et-jc-literature-of-9-11-course-under-fire-20150901 -story.html.

7. *Dariano v. Morgan Hill Unified School District,* United States Court of Appeals for the Ninth Circuit, filed February 27, 2014, accessed October 22, 2015, http://www.americanfreedom lawcenter.org/wp-content/uploads/2012/02/11-17858.pdf.

Preparation #13
Take Back the Rainbow

1. GilbertBaker.com, accessed October 17, 2015, http://gilbertbaker.com/GILBERT_BAKER _ORIGINAL_COLORS/BIO.html.

2. Pew Research Center, "Changing Attitudes on Gay Marriage," July 29, 2015, accessed October 18, 2015, http://www.pewforum.org/2015/07/29/graphics-slideshow-changing -attitudes-on-gay-marriage/.

3. Michael L. Brown, *A Queer Thing Happened to America: And What a Long, Strange Trip It's Been,* (Equal Time Books, 2011), 18–19.

4. "The diagnostic status of homosexuality in DSM-III: a reformulation of the issues," *The American Journal of Psychiatry*, Volume 138 Issue 2, February 1981, pp. 210–215, accessed October 17, 2015, http://ajp.psychiatryonline.org/doi/abs/10.1176/ajp.138.2.210.

5. Michael L. Brown, *A Queer Thing Happened to America*, 36–40.

6. Marshall Kirk and Hunter Madsen, *After the Ball: How America Will Conquer Its Fear and Hatred of Gays in the 90s* (Plume, 1990), 153.

7. Brown, *A Queer Thing Happened to America*, 32.

8. Kirk and Madsen, *After the Ball*, 32.

9. Brown, *A Queer Thing Happened to America*, 48–51.

10. James R. Aist, "The Gay Agenda's 'Planned, Psychological Attack' on Straight America," *ChristianPost.com*, November 22, 2013, accessed October 17, 2015, http://ipost.christianpost .com/news/the-gay-agendas-planned-psychological-attack-on-straight-america-12488/?redirect.

11. Juliet Eilperin, "Critics pounce after Obama talks Crusades, slavery at prayer breakfast," *The Washngton Post*, February 5, 2015, accessed october 17, 2015, https://www.washingtonpost. com /politics/obamas-speech-at-prayer-breakfast-called-offensive-to-christians/2015/02/05/6a15a240 -ad50-11e4-ad71-7b9eba0f87d6_story.html.

12. Aist, "The Gay Agenda's 'Planned, Psychological Attack.'"

Preparation #14
Recognize Socialism and Communism

1. Rachael Kohn, "Progressive Christianity and the Bible: is belief causing the decline of faith?" *ABC.Net.au*, May 29, 2015, accessed October 17, 2015, http://www.abc.net.au/radionational /programs/spiritofthings/is-belief-causing-the-decline-of-faith/6504294.

2. John Bennison, "Defining Progressive Christianity: An Open-Ended 'Creed' for a Progressive Christian," *ProgressiveChristianity.org*, November 10, 2014, accessed October 17, 2015, http:// progressivechristianity.org/resources/defining-progressive-christianity/.

3. "Little Change in Public's Response to 'Capitalism,' 'Socialism'," *Pew Research Center*, January 10, 2012, accessed October 17, 2015, http://www.pewresearch.org/daily-number /little-change-in-publics-response-to-capitalism-socialism/.

10. Nick Corasaniti, "Bernie Sanders Makes Rare Appeal to Evangelicals at Liberty University," *NewYorkTimes.com*, September 14, 2015, accessed October 17, 2015, http://www.nytimes.com /politics/first-draft/2015/09/14/bernie-sanders-makes-rare-appeal-to-evangelicals-at-liberty -university/?_r=0.

Preparation #15
Investigate the Islam Question for Yourself

1. Yassin Musharbash, "The Future of Terrorism: What al-Qaida Really Wants," *Spiegel Online International*, August 12, 2005, accessed October 17, 2015, http://www.spiegel.de/international /the-future-of-terrorism-what-al-qaida-really-wants-a-369448.html#spRedirectedFrom=www&r eferrrer=http://pamelageller.com/2015/03/pamela-geller-wnd-islamic-caliphate-by-2020.html/.

2. Graeme Wood, "What ISIS Really Wants," *The Atlantic*, March 2015, accessed October 17, 2015, http://www.theatlantic.com/magazine/archive/2015/03/what-isis-really-wants/384980/.

3. Kellan Howell, "Islamic State Supporters Claim New Caliphate in Europe: 'Convert or Die'," *The Washington Times*, October 16, 2015, accessed October 17, 2015, http://m.washington times.com/news/2015/oct/16/islamic-state-supporters-claim-new-caliphate-europ/.

4. "Sunni rebels declare new 'Islamic caliphate,'" *Aljazeera*, June 30, 2014, accessed October 17, 2015, http://www.aljazeera.com/news/middleeast/2014/06/isil-declares-new-islamic-caliphate -201462917326669749.html.

5. Anugrah Kumar, "Ben Carson on Muslim President: I'll Change My Position If You Show Me Islamic Text Opposed to Shariah," *The Christian Post*, September 28, 2015, accessed October 17, 2015, http://www.christianpost.com/news/ben-carson-on-muslim-president-ill -change-my-position-if-you-show-me-islamic-text-opposed-to-sharia-146316/.

6. Samantha Page, "Ben Carson Says He'd Consider Religion As Probable Cause For Searches," *ThinkProgress.org*, September 27, 2015, accessed October 17, 2015, http://thinkprogress.org /politics/2015/09/27/3706095/carson-islam-probable-cause/.

7. Yassin Musharbash, "Islamophobia is racism, pure and simple," *The Guardian*, December 10, 2014, accessed October 17, 2015, http://www.theguardian.com/commentisfree/2014/dec/10 /islamophobia-racism-dresden-protests-germany-islamisation.

8. Terri Rupar, "Here are the ten countries where homosexuality may be punished by death," *The Washington Post*, February 24, 2014, accessed October 17, 2015, https://www.washington post.com/news/worldviews/wp/2014/02/24/here-are-the-10-countries-where-homosexuality -may-be-punished-by-death/.

9. Mark A. Gabriel, *Islam and Terrorism* (Lake Mary, FL: Frontline, 2002).

10. Dave Boucher, "Lawmakers Fear Islamic 'Indoctrination' in Schools," *The Nashville Tennesseean*, September 10, 2015, accessed October 17, 2015, http://www.usatoday.com/story /news/nation/2015/09/10/lawmakers-fear-islamic-indoctrination-schools/72038416/.

11. Kristine Marsh, "Nets Hype Muslims Targeted In Chapel Hill Shootings 12 Times More Than Christians In Oregon," FoxNews.Com, October 9, 2015, accessed October 17, 2015, http://nation.foxnews.com/2015/10/09/nets-hype-muslims-targeted-chapel-hill-shootings-12 -times-more-christians-oregon.

12. Office of the Press Secretary, "Remarks by the President at Cairo University, 6-04-09," *The White House,* June 4, 2009, accessed October 17, 2015, https://www.whitehouse.gov/the-press -office/remarks-president-cairo-university-6-04-09.

13. Pew Research Center, "America's Changing Religious Landscape," accessed October 17, 2015, http://www.pewforum.org/2015/05/12/americas-changing-religious-landscape/.

14. SpearIt, "Raza Islamica: Prisons, Hip Hop & Converting Converts" (February 11, 2013). *Berkeley La Raza Law Journal*, Vol. 22, No. 1, 2012, accessed October 17, 2015, http://papers .ssrn.com/sol3/papers.cfm?abstract_id=1652121.

Preparation #16
Debrief Your Team

1. Laura Mae Gardner, Howie Bowman, and Keån Williams, "Debriefing in Mission Settings," *Barnabas.org*, accessed October 18, 2015, https://www.barnabas.org/files/Debriefing%20in%20 Missions%20Settings.pdf.

Preparation #17
Restore the Family Altar

1. Martin Luther and Walther I. Brandt, tr., *The Estate of Marriage*, 1522, accessed online October 18, 2015, https://www.1215.org/lawnotes/misc/marriage/martin-luther-estate-of -marriage.pdf.

2. *The Lutheran Witness, Official Periodical of The Lutheran Church—Missouri Synod* (St.Louis, Concordia Publishing House, October 2015).

3. John Knox, *The Daily Exercise of God's Most Holy & Sacred Word*, 1557.

4. Thomas Manton, *Epistle to the Reader of the Westminster Confession of Faith and Larger and Shorter Catechisms*, 1646.

5. Matthew Henry, *A Church in the House or Family Religion*, 1704.

6. George Whitefield, *Sermon 4: The Great Duty of Family Religion*, 1738.

7. Jonathan Edwards, *A Farewell Sermon,* 1750.

8. C. H. Spurgeon, *A Pastoral Visit,* 362–363, 1908.

9. *The Book of Common Prayer*, 1928.

Preparation #19
Learn From the Real Heroes

1. Caitlyn Jenner accepted the Arthur Ashe Courage Award at the ESPYS on July 15, 2015, accessed October 10, 2015, http://espn.go.com/espys/2015/story/_/id/13264599/caitlyn -jenner-accepts-arthur-ashe-courage-award-espys-ashe2015.

2. Dave Boyer, "Obama 'proud' of openly gay basketball player," *The Washington Times*, April 30, 2013, accessed October 10, 2015, http://www.washingtontimes.com/news/2013/apr/30 /obama-proud-openly-gay-basketball-player/.

3. "Ellen DeGeneres Awards," Internet Movie Database, accessed October 18, 2015, http:// www.imdb.com/name/nm0001122/awards.

4. Lisa Respers France, "God and the movies: How 'War Room' is winning the battle of the box office," CNN.Com, accessed October 10, 2015, http://www.cnn.com/2015/09/08 /entertainment/war-room-box-office-feat/.

5. "Ben Carson Biography," Biography.com, accessed October 10, 2015, http://www.biography .com/people/ben-carson-475422.

Preparation #20
Ephesians 5 Your Life

1. Commonsensemedia.org accessed October 10, 2015, https://www.commonsensemedia.org /tv-reviews/game-of-thrones.

2. Michael Brown, "From 'Leave It to Beaver' to 'Game of Thrones,'" Townhall.com, accessed October 10, 2015, http://townhall.com/columnists/michaelbrown/2015/09/24/from-leave-it -to-beaver-to-game-of-thrones-n2056447/page/full.

3. John H. McWhorter, "How Dare You Say That! The Evolution of Profanity," *The Wall Street Journal*, July 17, 2015, accessed October 10, 2015, http://www.wsj.com/articles/how-dare-you -say-that-the-evolution-of-profanity-1437168515.

4. Ibid.

Preparation #21
Dump the Stress...No Really!

1. Marie Kondo, *The Life-Changing Magic of Tidying Up: The Japanese Art of Decluttering and Organizing,* Ten Speed Press, 2014.

2. Horatio G. Spafford, *It Is Well With My Soul,* 1873.

Preparation # 23
Avoid the "Most Disturbing Church Trend of All"

1. Will Mancini, "The Most Disturbing Church Trend of Them All," Charismanews.com, January 12, 2015, accessed October 11, 2015, http://www.charismanews.com/us/47835 -the-most-disturbing-church-trend-of-them-all.

2. Ibid.

3 Ibid.

4. Josh Packard Ph.D, and Ashleigh Hope, *Church Refugees: Sociologists reveal why people are DONE with church but not their faith*, Group Publishing, 2015.

5. "Joseph Juran," *The Economist*, June, 2009. accessed October 11, 2015, http://www .economist.com/node/13881008.

ABOUT THE AUTHOR

Lisa Cherry tackles sticky issues with sensitivity and courage. Her passion for truth is second only to her passion for Jesus. As an author, speaker, and mom, she loves to mine the wisdom of the Word of God and impart these life-changing truths to today's generation.

She and her husband, Doug, along with their children, founded Frontline Family Ministries, POTTS (Parents of Teens and Tweens), Victory Dream Center (an outreach urban ministry church), and REALITY Youth Center. She travels nationwide speaking to parents, churches, women, teens, and leaders.

After nearly losing her daughter Kalyn to a crazy case of sexual abuse, Lisa learned firsthand the dangers of the dark flood. She and Kalyn are authors of *Unmask the Predators: The Battle to Protect Your Child*. Lisa and her son Lucas authored *Not Open: Win the Invisible Spiritual Culture War*.

Lisa has been interviewed on national programs such as CBN.com, Moody Radio, LeSEA Broadcasting, American Family Radio, The Lighthouse Report, Women Today Radio, The USA Network, and more.

She and her husband, Doug are parents of ten children, grandparents of six, and make their home in southern Illinois.

Church & Women's Ministry Campaigns!

Help prepare those you care about.

Use our *LIKE A FLOOD* campaign pack to help lead others into a new season of readiness for the DARK FLOOD sweeping across our nation and the BEAUTIFUL FLOOD riding on the waves of God's mercy and grace.

The campaign pack includes:

- Teaching/Preaching Outlines
- Video Sessions
- Self-Assessment Tests
- Customizable Publication Media Pack
- 30-day Reading Plan
- 30-day Journaling Plan
- Posters
- Discussion Points

This is a great way for pastors and leaders to help their people navigate the difficult waters raging around us.

Lisa and her team are ready to design a customized event for your group.

Visit www.FrontlineFamilies.org or call 800-213-9899 or email info@FrontlineFamilies.org for the campaign pack or for more information.

Also contact us about having Lisa come and speak at your event.

www.FrontlineFamilies.org

FrontLine Family Ministries

Growing spiritual and healthy families!

- Project 7000
- Daily online tips for parents
- Resources for parents and teens
- Timely topics for families
- Books, workbooks, e-books, DVDs, CDs, podcasts, articles, etc.

- Lisa's blog
- Prayer support
- Parent coaching
- Conferences and events

To schedule Doug, Lisa, Kalyn, Lucas, Hannah, or another Frontline Families speaker to speak at your church, parent organization, women's conference, youth event, or special event:

Call **800.213.9899**.

Email **booking@FrontlineFamilies.org**
or **Lisa@FrontlineFamilies.org**.

Visit **www.FrontlineFamilies.org**.

Other Resources from FrontLine

FrontLine
Family Ministries

Curriculum Kit
Book | 10 Session DVD
10 Session CD | Discussion Guide

PARENTS OF TEENS AND TWEENS

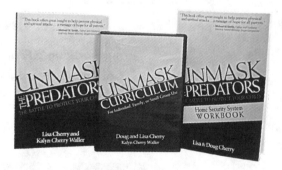

Individual Resources